D1400137

ALL OUT
FOR FREEDOM

HERO STORIES

FROM THE SECOND

WORLD WAR

SELECTED AND EDITED

BY MARIAN RHOADS

GINN AND COMPANY

BOSTON · NEW YORK · CHICAGO · ATLANTA
DALLAS · COLUMBUS · SAN FRANCISCO · TORONTO · LONDON

FOREWORD

Every war has produced its heroes and written its stories. The far-flung conflict of our time is unique in that modern means of transportation and communication and modern styles of news-writing have made possible vivid, personalized, "on the spot" records, which come to us with a speed hitherto unknown. We can go behind the scenes, so to speak. We can taste danger and hardship, trials and triumphs. We can see men and machines in action. We can learn again the meaning of individual daring, courage, perseverance, ingenuity, and real teamwork.

The purpose of this collection is to preserve some of these stories as sources of pride and patriotism. The selections included have been chosen chiefly for their story interest and variety. Many of them come from the fighting fronts all over the world. None of them, to my knowledge, was written before 1942.

A large number of the stories are about planes—the bombing of Japanese ships in the Pacific, dog-fighting in the skies of China with the famous Flying Tigers, the first spectacular flight over Tokyo, the organization of a large-scale bombing raid. Here are the experiences of dropping through the skies by parachute, of night fighting, of a ferry pilot's encounter with a tornado, of a wounded R.A.F. pilot, of what it feels like to be dive-bombed by Stukas. But we have not permitted planes entirely to steal the show. Here, too, are stories of submarine warfare, of gallant ground fighting, of the daring deeds of the

Commandos, of tank-testing, and stories from the home front of production and of scrap. As the very nature of the conflict requires, some of these stories are of other nations which are joined with us in this global war to preserve man's freedom.

It has seemed important to save the individuality and intensity of these stories. Editing, therefore, has been confined to certain omissions, to a few changes of vocabulary, and to introductions.

I wish again to express my gratitude to those individuals and organizations whose permission to use their material has made this book possible; likewise to *Time* magazine, which proved a valuable reference in writing several of the introductions.

MARIAN RHOADS

CONTENTS

vi

Yesterday, December 7, 1941—a date which will live in infamy—the United States of America was suddenly and deliberately attacked by naval and air forces of the Empire of Japan. . . . Always will our whole nation remember the character of the onslaught against us. . . . No matter how long it may take us to overcome this premeditated invasion, the American people in their righteous might will win through to absolute victory. . . . We will not only defend ourselves to the uttermost but will make it very certain that this form of treachery shall never again endanger us. . . . We will gain the inevitable triumph—so help us God. I ask that the Congress declare . . . a state of war.

ALL OUT
FOR FREEDOM

SECRET MISSION TO NORTH AFRICA

Excerpt from a broadcast by *Lowell Thomas*[1]

On November 8, 1942, a "powerful American force" supported by British sea and air forces landed on the Atlantic and Mediterranean coasts of French Africa. Its purpose was to prevent action in that part of the world by the aggressor nations and to aid Russia. The entire undertaking was under the high command of an American, Lieutenant General Dwight Eisenhower of the United States Army. Within a week President Roosevelt sent a message of congratulations to General Eisenhower and to every member of his command for "the highly successful accomplishment of a most difficult task." The African operations involved the transportation of thousands of troops through enemy-infested waters. Preceding them was a vast amount of planning, of training of troops, and of diplomacy. As the hour for the action drew near one more task remained—someone had to go to North Africa to establish firsthand contacts with pro-Allied sympathizers and to obtain vital military information. Here is that epic story, "an adventure story of war and high politics," as told by Lowell Thomas.

While the American offensive was in process of secret preparation, a group of high French officers in North Africa made a pretty good guess of what was coming. Though in the service of the Vichy Government, they were anti-Nazi and secretly favored the cause of the United Nations. Among them were representatives of General

[1]Excerpt from Lowell Thomas's broadcast, November 12, 1942. Used with the permission of the author.

3

Giraud, the famous French Commander who escaped from Nazi Germany. Giraud in Vichy-controlled France wanted to join in some action against the Nazis and through representatives in Africa he was inquiring about the possibilities.

The group of patriotic Frenchmen got in touch with American representatives, and suggested that an American general be sent secretly to meet them at Algiers—an undercover mission. This word was transmitted to the War Department in Washington where it was okayed.

As the General to lead the undercover mission, the War Department selected Major General Mark W. Clark— forty-six years old, slim and sharp eyed, an able soldier and an astute diplomat. In underground contact with the French officers whom they were to meet, General Clark arranged a trip that would make the thrills of a mystery novel seem pale. Much of the story of how they went is a military secret. Today, in North Africa, General Clark said, "I used planes, trains, ships, submarines, canoes, automobiles—and everything but mules."

The melodramatic high spot came when they finally made their way to Algiers—and here we are reminded of the immortal Paul Revere, who caught the signal of a light from a church tower. It had been arranged that when they got to a certain point along the Algerian coast, they would get a signal in the form of a light in the window of a house.

When they arrived on a pre-arranged night, however, the light was not there. What was wrong? General Clark and his companions were afraid they had been led into a trap. But they waited until the next night, kept

4

in hiding, subsisting on the food they had brought with them. Late the next night, as they kept their eyes glued on the house—a flash suddenly pierced the darkness, a light in a window. They went to the place, which was in almost complete darkness except for the signal. A man greeted them, the owner of the house. He told them that to preserve secrecy he had sent his wife away—also his Arab servants, giving them a few days off.

The Americans were led inside. "The house," General Clark related today, "was filled with French military officers in uniform—although they had come to the place in civilian clothes." Meaning they had journeyed to the rendezvous in civilian clothes for secrecy, but wore their uniforms during the conference to give it a more official status.

"We conferred all day and all night, until we had gathered all the information we wanted," says General Clark. They gathered plenty. The French officers agreed to collaborate with the forthcoming American offensive. They gave to the Americans complete plans of all French military installations in North Africa, the disposition of troops, the type of equipment and garrisons, and data on what French leaders could be counted on as friendly. They even made an arrangement to have the airfields outside Algiers delivered over to General Jimmy Doolittle's air force, when the offensive began. An agreement was made with representatives of General Giraud. Today, at the War Department in Washington, the following was stated: "In this conference, Clark opened negotiations which brought about the collaboration of Giraud with the United Nations."

5

Adding it all up—the secret mission headed by General Clark laid all the important ground work for the invasion of French North Africa.

The conference a complete success—there was a break of bad luck that nearly resulted in the ruin of everything. The secret meeting was nearly discovered—the Americans were within a hair's breadth of being detected and arrested by the Vichy authorities.

The Arab servants who had been given several days off grew suspicious. They went to the Vichy police and gave them the tip. The conference was just being completed, when word came—the police were on their way. Luckily, there were anti-Nazi elements among the police —and they sent the warning.

"I never saw such excitement in my life," General Clark laughed today. "Maps disappeared like lightning. A French General in military uniform changed into civilian clothes in one minute flat. I last saw him going out of a window. They were going in all directions."

General Clark and his group of Americans gathered their papers and equipment—the vital information that had been given to them. And they ducked down into an empty wine cellar. Hiding there, they could hear the arrival of the police, and the talk between the Vichy henchmen and the owner of the house.

As they crouched in the darkness, one of the officers was seized with an almost uncontrollable desire to cough. "I am afraid," he whispered, "that if I hold this cough back any longer, I am going to choke to death."

They expected that at any minute the police would come down into the cellar. General Clark crouched with his revolver in his hand. "If the police came down, I was undecided whether to shoot them or bribe them. I had fifteen thousand francs in my pocket." But the Vichy police did not think about the cellar, and after hanging around for an hour, they left. So now the Americans were able to be on their way. They had accomplished their mission, had got the goods. They went down to the shore where boats awaited them—got aboard and started away from the shore. But the boats upset, and they were thrown into the water. General Clark lost his pants, and the others lost their clothes, but that wasn't all. "I lost some eighteen thousand dollars in gold," the General said. And he laughed: "I wonder if Morgenthau will get after me for that."

But they managed to save their papers—the invaluable data for the great offensive. They got ashore and, in their under-clothing, hid all day in a patch of woods, cold and shivering. At length, anti-Nazi agents got in touch with them, and they were taken out of North Africa—to report what they had accomplished.

Lieutenant General Eisenhower stated today, "The fact that land resistance was not terrifically great anywhere and that we did not have to land any place where opposition was great—testifies to the success of the Clark mission." And General Eisenhower added, "It was a modern message to Garcia."

And today President Roosevelt promoted Major General Clark to the rank of Lieutenant General!

PARACHUTING WITH THE SUPER-COMMANDOS

By *Gordon Gaskill*. By cable from Cairo[1]

A lowly Scottish subaltern was sent to the Middle East with the famous Commandos. One day he had an idea. From the Commandos he wanted to choose an even more carefully picked group and organize them into a small, supertrained band, capable of going anywhere, even by parachute, and doing anything. His idea met with approval, and today he is one of the youngest majors in the British Army. For a long time military censorship kept the activities of the paratroops veiled. Then the capture of one of their planes with some of these Super-Commandos and all the equipment which the wounded men were unable to destroy gave away their secret to the Germans. Mr. Gaskill tells us some of their adventures and gives us an idea of what it is like to parachute from a plane. Later you will read another story, "The Fighting-est Outfit in the British Army—The Commandos." Both these stories about British Commandos show that the United States Rangers and the Junior Commandos of the United States have a tradition of gallant daring to be proud of.

The Italian commandant was frantic. The world had gone mad tonight. He couldn't believe his eyes, still fogged by sleep, for it was three o'clock in the morning. His airdrome garrison town seemed to be under heavy attack and half of it was already blazing.

[1]From *The American Magazine*, July, 1942, "Toughest Job in the War," by Gordon Gaskill. Used with the permission of the author. Copyright, 1942, The Crowell-Collier Publishing Company.

His bewildered brain told him that it was impossible. The British were at least 250 miles away, no planes had been sighted, and surely they couldn't. . . . The gasoline dump went up with a mighty roar. One by one a line of airplanes began exploding into flames, apparently by themselves.

The commandant almost sobbed; the planes had been brand-new.

His 800 troops were running about wild and witless. They carried rifles and submachine guns, but had no targets. So they fired everywhere—at anything—at everything—at nothing. Ghosts and devils were abroad tonight. The commandant saw that they were in complete panic.

So was he. He rushed a message to the next garrison. "Under heavy attack. Must have immediate help. Unable to hold out much longer."

Crouching in the wadi at the edge of the airdrome, peering happily through the desert scrub at the havoc they had caused, were the attacking British forces. Neither ghosts nor devils, they consisted of exactly two men—a young Scottish major and a cockney sergeant. They belonged to a little known fighting group which, for bold imagination and courage, cannot be excelled anywhere on earth—British parachute troops of the Middle East.

The attack, so terrible and supernatural to the Italians, seemed quite simple to them. They had merely tiptoed about the airdrome in the dead of night, depositing little sixteen-ounce, delayed-action bombs here and there, in any likely place—in gasoline stores, airplane cockpits, bomb piles. Then they had crept away in the darkness to hide. It would take thirty minutes for the bombs to begin exploding. They had plenty of time to get away later. They wanted to see the fun.

Commandos are super-soldiers, while the Mid-East's paratroops are super-commandos. Their training and equipment have been thought out to the most exact details. Even things which seem far-fetched and ridiculous have proved their worth in battle.

Once returning from a raid on foot, a body of paratroops were spotted by a German Messerschmitt, which darted down to machine-gun them. They were in perfectly flat desert with no place to hide. Each man brought out a bit of burlap, dug a shallow hole in the sand, pulled the burlap over him, sprinkled sand on top, and crawled in. As far as the Messerschmitt was concerned, they simply disappeared.

Another returning party had only one quart of water for five men. They almost died of thirst until they reached the sea. Here they hooked together two water bottles with thirty-inch rubber tubing which each man carried, boiled salt water in the first bottle, and condensed fresh water in the second. It took five hours to make one quart, but it saved their lives.

The paratroops have their own special bomb. It looks like a handful of soft, black putty and can be molded into any shape, as it never hardens. It can be fused to go off instantly, or in any desired time up to two and a half hours. It is a combination of high explosive and thermite. The first blows things up, while the second sets anything, even metal, afire. It weighs only one pound, and each man easily carries at least a dozen.

The paratroops have had extraordinary luck. Once

while sneaking away from an enemy airdrome after laying their eggs, they suddenly saw an enemy truck driving toward them with blazing headlights. In a few seconds the lights would have picked them out plainly. Just then one of their own bombs exploded back on the airdrome and the enemy driver, thinking there was an air raid on, instantly doused his lights and swept by, without seeing them.

Other incidents which appear to be nothing but luck are really something more. Like the time when the paratroops were creeping along an enemy building in the darkness. Suddenly a window above them opened, and an Italian looked out. They were plainly visible in the light flooding down on them. One paratrooper pointed a tommy gun at the Italian but didn't fire. The Italian muttered something and closed the window. A British officer who understood Italian explained later: The man had thought they were his own blackout patrol and had apologized for letting so much light show! This is not luck; it is the very basis of paratroop theory. As the major explained it to me, "The enemy never expects you in his own back yard."

One night a few paratroops went to sleep in what they thought was an empty desert. In the morning when they awoke they found themselves smack in the middle of a German encampment, not fifty paces from the German colonel's tent. Their first thought was of trying to sneak away, but it was broad daylight and the ground was bare. So they packed up calmly and strolled off. They walked straight through the German camp, dressed in British uniforms, and nobody paid any attention to them.

11

It sounds strange, but sometimes parachute troops don't use parachutes.

In the desert, which is like the ocean, it's possible to drive almost anywhere with a truck without being spotted if you make wide detours and drive the ticklish stretches by night. Thus paratroops often fall in line with a moving enemy convoy at night. They soon learn the headlight recognition signals and blink as cheerfully as any Jerry. They park in enemy parking lots. If they need food, water, or gas, they merely cut one enemy truck out of the convoy or encampment and hold it up.

The primary object of the paratroop raids is to destroy vital enemy equipment and spread panic, but often they run across a large mess building or tent in the dark and can't resist the temptation to have a go at it. "We just act as if we belong there," a lieutenant said in telling me about a raid he made with a cockney private. "We were walking across this airdrome when we saw a big building. Little cracks of light were leaking out, and inside we could hear Germans singing and talking. We didn't say a word but began walking toward the building. The private had a tommy gun with two extra magazines, and I had a .45 and two extra clips. As we got nearer, we realized there were a lot of men inside and the private whispered, "Oh, lovely," and we nearly burst out laughing. I yanked the door open, and we both began firing. I'll never forget the looks on their faces. They simply stared. Not a single person ever fired back. I suppose we killed about fifty, mostly officers. I remember the private yelling as we ran away, "That's for London, you ——— so-and-so's!"

So far the paratroops have operated only with handfuls of men; no more than ten have ever gone out on a raid. They believe ten can do nearly as much vital damage as two hundred and run much less risk of detection, and they prefer five to ten—"five good men." I know a lieutenant who took four men on a raid to an important enemy drome and destroyed twenty-four planes in one night. Nine nights later he did exactly the same thing at exactly the same airdrome and got twenty-seven more, a total of fifty-one planes in nine days. Another group of five men burned up thirty-seven planes in one night for the largest single bag. In each case, all got back safely by disappearing into the trackless desert in the darkness and later meeting with trucks.

Some have lain as long as three days and nights beside enemy airdromes, noting vital targets and watching in amusement the enemy taking anti-paratroop precautions every evening. Sometimes the Italians have put out so many sentries they could almost join hands, and other times stationed sentries at each plane, all to no avail. Paratroops get in anyway.

A sergeant took me under his wing when I made a thousand-foot practice jump with them. I climbed into a converted bomber with fourteen others, and like them wore a crash helmet and coverall uniform, heavy high-laced boots, and knee protectors. As we circled up to a thousand feet, the sergeant kept explaining how to try to land in a relaxed half-sitting position and not worry if another parachute drifted into me. "They just kiss and float apart like two balloons," he explained.

A red "get-ready" light winked, and he showed me how to hook one end of my parachute cord onto a ring

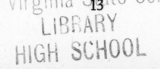
13

which slid on a greased steel rod running lengthwise down the cabin.

Then a green light flashed, and the lieutenant in command went first.

The men jumped faster than one per second, and I went leaping out the door before I realized it. The line tied to the plane dragged the chute from the pack; then when my full weight hit the extended line, the connection broke, and I fell free. There was no sharp jerk. It was the most exhilarating sensation I've ever known as I seemed to hang motionless in heaven in a great silence. It was so still I could talk in almost conversational tones to other men drifting down around me.

I began swinging like a pendulum. Then the sergeant said, "Here comes the ground." Previously I had felt as if I were standing still, but now suddenly the ground came into focus, rushing up at terrific speed. Actually we were dropping seventeen feet per second, and it took only sixty seconds to reach the ground. I was swinging widely as I struck and tumbled head over heels twice. The chute began dragging me. I dimly remembered some advice about this, and finally recalled that there was a release knob on my chest. I turned it, and the chute fell away. Then I sat down. It had been a hard jolt but I was unhurt. I ran my hands into soft, warm sand, and I felt very good.

A practice jump like that is one thing; a battle jump is quite another. That day was perfectly clear, and the spot was chosen especially because the sand was the softest. You knew what you were jumping into and when you would hit, but on the first battle jump the paratroops

*A British paratrooper about to land. Mr. Gaskill describes
how he may have felt coming down*

A paratrooper helps to secure a comrade's parachute

Action to keep sea lanes clear. A depth bomb seeks a lurking submarine[1]

[1]Reprinted by special permission of the *Saturday Evening Post*; copyright by the Curtis Publishing Company, 1942.

One of the famous United States Flying Fortresses. A Flying Fortress helped Colonel Sweeney to find the Japs

made, it was one of the worst nights North Africa has known. Rain was splashing down in icy sheets in total darkness. Even on the ground the wind was a thirty-mile gale, murderous to parachutists. It was the worst possible night, but paratroops had orders to jump at all costs, so they did.

The sergeant who had taught me to jump was lost that night.

I can think of no greater courage. On their caps the paratroops wear a winged dagger with the words, "Who dares, wins."

They are doing both.

WE FOUND THE JAPS

By *Lieutenant Colonel Walter C. Sweeney, Jr.* From
United States Army Air Corps Headquarters, Hawaii[1]

On the afternoon of June 3, 1942, Navy patrol planes sighted
a Japanese fleet of about thirty ships some six hundred miles
west of Midway. From Midway Lieutenant Colonel Walter C.
Sweeney, Jr., of the United States Army Air Corps, led three
Flying Fortresses to the attack and scored hits on a heavy
cruiser and a transport so large that "one of the boys described
it as of the *Normandie* class." The battle continued from June
3 to 7, and from it came many proud tales of skill, heroism, and
success. Final figures showed that in this engagement the
enemy lost four aircraft carriers, two heavy cruisers, three destroyers, and a cargo vessel. Two or three battleships, three or
four heavy cruisers, one light cruiser, and four transports were
damaged. There were losses by the United States, but they
were small in comparison with those of the enemy. Lieutenant
Colonel Sweeney describes the action of his unit on the second
day of the engagement.

Early Thursday the entire squadron went off the
ground before dawn.

We decided to continue the attack on the ships which
some of our planes had pasted the previous evening.

But while we were on the way to our objective, we
received word that another Japanese invasion fleet, including carriers, had been spotted by Navy patrol boats.

We changed our course and headed for the new quarry.

[1]Used with the permission of United Press Associations, Inc.

Thanks to the work of our navigator, Lieutenant Bill Adams, San Bernardino, California, we found the Japs just where the PBY's had told us they were.

We saw the ships lined in two columns with their destroyers and lighter craft flanking the heavier capital ships. We paid no attention to them. We were after the carriers, which we knew would be farther back behind the main units.

The big, fluffy clouds made visibility difficult, and the Japanese carriers tried to hide under them.

But we spotted them way down below through a hole in the clouds. There were two of them in sight. I concentrated on one which was circling around and around, the typical Japanese defense maneuver against high level bombing attacks.

We were greeted by a hail of anti-aircraft fire which flowered all round us, like big black puff balls.

Make no mistake, those gunners were good. They put up a real curtain of fire around the carrier.

Just then Zero fighters came up to attack us, and, believe me, things were pretty hot up there for a few minutes.

We swung around into bombing position with high explosives bursting all over the place, and the Zeros banging away at us.

The carrier's decks were empty. We found out later its planes at that moment were attacking Midway.

Our element (three planes) went down out of the sun for the run over the target.

The doors of the bombing compartment swung open and over we went.

We laid our bombs right smack across the port bow, and we headed for home as fast as our motors would carry us.

I could not see the effects of our bombs immediately, but the tail gunner yelled over the interphone, "We got her right on the nose!"

I looked down as we banked around. Sure enough the entire bow of the carrier was belching smoke and flames. Even from our high altitude we could see that the carrier had been badly hit. The Japanese fighters gave us little trouble. They seemed to be more interested in the carrier than in us, and we soon lost them.

We started a second attack as soon as we had been refueled. We saw two ships burning as we flew out. One was a carrier and the other was a capital ship [battleship]. Both were about twenty miles behind the main body of the Japanese, who were fleeing in a general westward direction.

We could not find the other carriers, in spite of our intense search, so we picked out the biggest ship in the flock, which I judge was either a battleship or a heavy cruiser.

We were not bothered by Zeros, but the anti-aircraft barrage was as heavy as any I ever want to go through.

We had the sun pretty well at our backs as we made a run across the big ship, which apparently sensed that we had picked it out as a victim.

The ship was traveling at full speed, twisting and turning and making every possible maneuver to throw us off. Its wake looked like a piece of wrinkled ribbon on a blue background.

That run was just about as nearly perfect a bombing run as it was possible to obtain. Our pattern bombs smashed into the ship near the stern and sent a great puff of black oily smoke and a huge jet of flame bursting from its stern.

We did not hang round to watch but high-tailed it home, using the fires of crippled Japanese ships as beacons with which to get our bearings.

IN TOKYO BAY

By *Robert J. Casey*[1]

The scene, the launching of a Japanese carrier. In peace-time she had been a big and beautiful Japanese ocean liner. Now brown slant eyes gazed admiringly at her new lines and measured the force which she could throw against the white man. There was a brass band. Some admirals were there, too, for it was a gala event. But there was an uninvited—and, as it turned out, very important—guest. Like many other adventurous tales of submarines, this one was not told till many months after it had occurred and had become past history to its crew. You will find it good reading.

In those early days of the war one of our submarines went into Tokyo Bay. Having entered and reconnoitered the complicated shipping of Yokohama, the commander of the submarine picked out a suitable spot and sat down on the bottom.

It is customary, of course, for submarines to lie submerged in daylight and come up at night to change air and charge batteries. This one arose from its bed according to custom, and the commander, glancing about him in the moonlight, found himself squarely in front of a shipyard. And on the ways, only a few hundred yards distant was a big ship—a liner like the *Yawata*, maybe, or bigger. And it was obvious even in the halflight that

[1]Somewhat condensed and edited. Used by special permission of The Chicago Daily News Foreign Service. Copyright, 1942, The Chicago Daily News, Inc.

workmen had been trimming the superstructure to make an aircraft carrier out of her.

The commander looked and very nearly shed a tear. What you do in a case like this was something he'd never found out. To sink a ship like this one would be worth the trip across the Pacific. But you don't toss torpedoes up onto dry land, and you can't sink ships with no water under them.

By morning the problem was still unsolved. The sub went back to the bottom to rest during the heat of the day.

So went the routine for quite a long time. The commander maneuvered about until he found a spot where he could stick up a periscope during daylight hours. He edged about until he was at a favorable firing angle. But all to no end. The big ship, daily getting to look more and more like a carrier, stood out of the water and far beyond the reach of torpedoes. Daily the commander looked. Daily the sub went down to its berth in the mud, the problem unsolved. . . . Thus for two weeks—and three—and a month. . . . The skipper's mouth, it is said, showed signs of slavering as he looked at the distant prize, and he tried to argue with the navigator that the calendar was wrong, that he'd been in Tokyo Bay only three weeks instead of four. But the time was at hand, of course, for him to go somewhere else. The supplies were going to need replacing shortly, and besides he had his march orders to go to some new place on a definite date.

"Very well," he told the navigator. "We'll pull out tonight."

Then he gave orders to ease the big ship toward the surface.

They say it was a gala day for this part of Japan. The overhaul of the big liner had been accomplished in a record time, as the United States commander might have testified if anybody had asked him. The officials of the yard were there—and a couple of admirals as anybody could see from their flags. And there was a brass band. What it was playing nobody in the United States is likely to find out until after the war. . . . You can't hear such things through a periscope.

At the proper moment somebody knocked out the blocks. Somebody smashed the bottle of sake—if that's the way they launch ships in Japan. The big ship started down the ways. . . . Just then the submarine came up. The periscope edged above water. The commander looked at the scene for one dumfounded, unbelieving second. Such luck, of course, just couldn't happen to anybody. . . .

The ship came down. The commander stuck his face to the telephone. As the carrier hit the water, he put two tin fish into it. It continued straight down. The most complete launching ever seen in Tokyo.

"Just as well we're moving," the commander is quoted as having said, as they slipped through the narrows and into the more friendly sea. "That ship took over our spot on the bottom."

THE FLYING TIGERS—DAREDEVILS
OF THE AIR

By *William Clemmens*[1]

For nearly five years Japanese planes had controlled the skies over China. Then one day, above the Yunnan hills, a mysterious little group of fighters struck back at the Jap. In four days that group—the American Volunteer Group—cost the Japanese air force more fighting planes than they had lost in their attack on Hawaii or in the course of a whole year of war in China. Outnumbered twenty to one, with no reserves, with old planes, and without support, the A.V.G.'s, or Flying Tigers, as they came to be known, piled up the staggering record of 286 Jap planes destroyed, and a like number probably destroyed, in seven months. Thirty-four Japanese planes went down for every P-40 that was lost. How the now famous Tigers did it under the training and inspiration of their dauntless leader, General Claire Chennault, is a great story of perseverance, skill, and courage. It will be long remembered.

A retired United States military pilot, ferrying a twin-engined Lend-Lease flying boat to Australia, came down on the glassy sea off Rangoon between raids early Christmas morning. He was not supposed to be there, but he was expected.

As he landed, a welcoming committee of six eagerly grabbed his ship's bowline and helped bring the big

[1]From *Collier's*, July 4, 1942, "How Chennault Kills Japs," by William Clemmens. Used with the permission of the author and *Collier's*. Copyright, 1942, The Crowell-Collier Publishing Company.

Catalina flying boat alongside the dock. They, too, were Americans, all of them in their early twenties. The sun was blazing, yet they were uniformed in heavy, high-altitude flying suits. Across the back of each uniform was the Chinese army crest and, in Chinese characters, the message, "This man is an American volunteer fighting for China. Give him all the help you can."

One of the six greeted the pilot as he jumped to the dock.

"We're from over the hills," he said. Then he added quickly, "Isn't that tracer stuff you've got aboard?"

The ferry pilot nodded.

"Sure could use some of that here," the group's spokesman said. "You've got to take that clear to Australia?"

The ferry pilot looked at him a moment. "Well, now. . ." he began; then, "You boys fighting Japs, too?"

"And how! The sky's full of 'em. But all we've got is standard ammunition. We're blowing those Japs full of holes but can't bring 'em down. Now, if we could borrow some of that tracer to set them on fire. . ."

The ferry pilot picked up his orders. "Funny thing. These don't say where I'm going. Military secret, I guess. But this ammunition must be to fight Japs with. . . ."

The six A.V.G.'s jumped to it as one man. Hardly was the last case ashore when the raid alarm sounded. Dumping their ammunition into a battered station wagon, the six rushed off in one direction. The ferry pilot took off in another. Hanging under a cloud, he saw the whole show.

Nine Jap bombers, flying high, were heading for Rangoon's docks, piled with Lend-Lease supplies. Six P-40

24

fighters, brightly painted to resemble sharks, climbed straight into the sky to a point a mile above the Japs. There, leveling off, they split up into pairs. In teams of two, diving in such perfect harmony that both machines seemed to be under the control of a single hand, the six little fighters weaved, rolled, slashed their way through the oncoming Jap formation.

Before the ferry pilot had to head off for his next port, he saw seven columns of black curling smoke trailing seven spiraling Japanese planes down into Martaban Bay. Openmouthed, he turned to his co-pilot, "Say, that's old Chennault up there."

Chennault wasn't there but the American ferry pilot had found the key to a mystery that was rattling the teeth of the Japanese high command. Three days before, a mysterious force had struck down from the China clouds, and Japan's first "invincible" air squadron was blown out of the sky above the Yunnan hills. On Christmas Eve, a thousand miles away a second squadron was wiped out near Rangoon. On that very Christmas dawn, an attacking force of forty escorted bombers was "exploded" before it ever reached its target. Nineteen of the forty bombers were sent crashing headlong into the jungles before they could even fire a shot.

Against the forces of the United States, of Britain, and the Dutch the Japanese had proved their "invincibility" in the air. Only one obstacle stood in the path of swift, easy victory. The Burmese heavens were full of "sharks." A mass attack by eighty bombers and pursuits, launched at Rangoon on Christmas Day, was torn to pieces before it could reach its target. In the next dawn, an entire regiment of Japanese bombers, hidden deep in the Thailand jungle, was destroyed before it could get off the ground. That same night a fleet of dark Japanese raiders, far up the Burma Road, was sucked into a whirlpool of sudden death.

It took the Japanese a long time to discover—and the world even longer to appreciate—that Japan was barred from the road to India not by a super air force of the United Nations but by the aerial wizardry of an almost forgotten schoolteacher from the Louisiana lowlands, a U. S. Army ex-pilot, Claire L. Chennault. With only a handful of young American volunteers, with old style fighting planes he had begged, with fuel he had borrowed and with ammunition he often had to steal, Chennault turned Japan's "easy" blitzkrieg of Burma into a major campaign.

Born in Commerce, Texas, on September 6, 1890, Claire Chennault was brought up by his cotton planter father to be a farmer. He studied scientific agriculture at Louisiana State University, and then, that he might pass on to others what he had learned, took a teaching course at the State Normal School. He was principal of a rural high school, was married, and the father of three boys when he enlisted in the United States Army in 1917. Graduated from Officers' Training School, he was still a ground officer in the aviation section of the Signal Corps at the time of the Armistice. But flying had already got into his blood and a year later, having won his wings, he was commissioned a lieutenant in the newly formed U. S. Army Air Corps.

A natural teacher, he combined his love of flying for flying's sake with a schoolmaster's orderly study of this new art. He saw service at every principal air base around

26

the United States and took his turn at all branches of the flying service. He liked the fast-flying, hard-hitting pursuit work best. It was in Hawaii, as commandant of the 19th Pursuit Squadron in 1929, that he began an exhaustive study of aerial tactics.

By night he calculated and plotted. By day he test-flew all the intricate patterns of which those early fighting planes were capable. From these he developed a revolutionary concept of aerial warfare.

But when Chennault tried to fit his new tactics into the traditional pattern of combat flying, they just would not mesh. General John F. Curry, Chennault's commandant at Maxwell Field, cited him as "one of the outstanding authorities on pursuit aviation, a fearless pilot, and an able leader."

Our every-man-for-himself method of combat flying, Chennault held, was a throwback not only to World War I but to King Arthur. A team of three pursuits could drive any six individual fighters out of the sky, he argued. And to convince the Air Corps, he took two of his squadron mates, tied their wings to his own, and the three of them flying as one man, tore the sky apart. The higher-ups, however, saw in his demonstration only a spectacular stunt.

Then, in 1937, Captain Claire L. Chennault was retired —because of deafness incurred in line of duty. But he did not stay settled long. His two teammates, Lieutenants J. H. Williamson and W. C. McDonald, Jr., also retired from the Air Corps, went to China to help train combat pilots. When word reached them in Nanking that an American air adviser was to be sent to China, they went to work. The generalissimo and Madame Chiang-Kai-shek, sponsors of Chinese aviation, were impressed. If Chennault cared to come, the job was his. Every day or so he received a note from one or the other of his flying partners, but each said in effect little more than, "You ought to come to China. You'll find it very interesting." Finally, the old squadron leader packed his bags. He couldn't be sure, but he thought he smelled a fight.

Shortly after Chennault's arrival, in July, 1937, Generalissimo Chiang-Kai-shek went to war with Japan. He thought he had six hundred first-line combat planes. By the time Chennault discovered that China had actually less than one hundred, the Japanese had already won mastery of the air.

Flight by flight, Chennault watched the Japs wipe out China's air force. There was no visible means of getting either planes or pilots. But Chennault would not give up.

Doggedly, he planned ahead. When he was not training the few pilots for whom China had planes, Chennault was studying Japan's air force. He catalogued the strength and weakness of every Jap plane. Chennault took Japan's plan of aerial warfare apart. He psychoanalyzed the Japanese pilot, memorized his book of "precepts," learned his reactions to an innumerable series of conditions. Before long, Chennault, the air leader without planes or pilots, could peer at the sky through a pair of field glasses and describe to an openmouthed audience of staff officers each detailed move that an attacking Japanese squadron would make before it actually made it.

All this, probably the most complete intelligence on Japanese air power outside the secret files of Tokyo and

Berlin, Chennault stored up against the day when China could strike back. Month after month, he planned and schemed for American planes and pilots and equipment.

Planes for China? Certainly. But there were none to be had. Priorities. Aid to Britain. Army procurement. Navy allotments. Planes for the Netherlands, the East Indies, Australia, Belgium, Norway, Sweden, Russia. Then one day a delivery order for one hundred of the old-type Curtiss P-40 pursuits, originally allocated to Sweden was cancelled.

Chennault got those one hundred planes. But his troubles had only begun. After months in transit, the planes arrived in China with no replacement parts. To start, then, he would have to keep half of them in the shops to supply spare parts to keep the other fifty in the air. They required a corps of skilled mechanics, which only America could supply. Their liquid-cooled engines demanded high-octane gasoline, as rare as gold in China. Their machine guns, six to each plane, needed an assortment of ammunition. Most serious of all, there were no pilots in China who could fly his fighters.

In one last desperate effort, Chennault, then a general in the Chinese army, returned to the United States. First he called at Washington, then visited air base after air base around the country. All he asked was permission to talk to the pilot group. He had no order, no letter of authority. Group after group heard about China, what the Chinese were up against, what could be done. China needed pilots, desperately. Each man would have to take his chances. But Chennault promised to give each man a cause worth fighting for.

29

One hundred pilots trailed Chennault from the camps —and a corps of airplane and engine mechanics, riggers, and armorers followed suit. From the forty-eight states, three hundred men were collected. They went as civilians, not as members of the Air Corps.

Chennault flew across the Pacific by clipper and met them at Rangoon. Across interior Burma, which was to be their future battleground, they were whisked into the school he had prepared at Toungoo. In simple, schoolmaster's language, he taught the youngsters all he knew of flying, all the little secrets he had learned about the Japs.

Chennault believes that a simple plan well carried out is far better than the most complex pattern poorly executed. His credo: teamwork; precision. He trained his youngsters as a top-flight coach would train a fast-moving basketball team. He drilled them on the tactics used by the British, Germans, Italians, French, Japanese, and Chinese, as well as on the American pattern. He required his A.V.G. cadets to practice six to eight hours a day on each maneuver until it was letter-perfect. Later, he would team them up in pairs and have them perform the same maneuvers until, in formation, they could execute the same precision as if every plane in the group were held by a single control.

Then, by precept and example, he taught them how to fight. His theory was simple. Japanese planes could climb faster, turn quicker, bring more fire power to bear. His P-40's had two points—and only two—on the credit side. They were speedier and sturdier; they could dive harder than the Japs. His plan of attack, then, was designed to maneuver the Japs into such a position that they would

*A flight leader of the Flying Tigers in one of the A.V.G. planes
painted to resemble a shark's head*

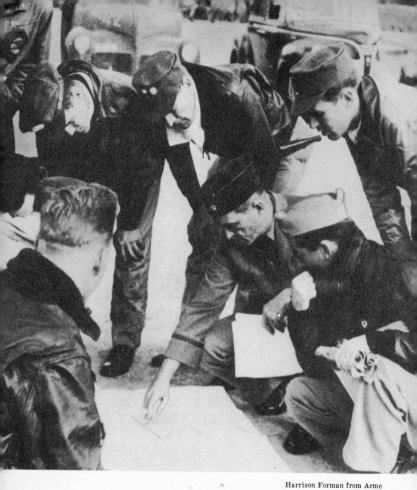

*General Claire Chennault, hand on map, discussing a mission
with his Flying Tigers*

Press Association, Inc.

For his achievement in downing five Jap planes in one day Lieutenant Edward O'Hare was made Lieutenant Commander and given the highest military award of the United States, the Congressional Medal of Honor

Acme

A glimpse of desert battle

have to reveal their weaknesses. Against these, he would pit his superior speed and strength. Above all, Chennault counted one great advantage: Japan, like the United States, Britain, even Germany, maneuvered according to the old traditional pattern of air combat. His boys were taught a new system—an attack by teams in wide, weaving strokes from above and below.

Beyond this, he gave them only five rules. First: never attack alone. One P-40 against one Jap is outnumbered three to one. But a team of two P-40's together can outhit, outfight any six Japanese. Second: get there first. Then you know where you are going to meet the enemy. He doesn't. Third: make your fire count. Your bullets have to run into the Jap. You can't count on him running into your bullets. Fourth: don't try to get them all at once. Strike one—with all you've got. Then head for home. Fifth: don't wait to see what will happen next—because it will happen to you.

It was in Toungoo that they painted the shark's head on the snout of the P-40's. The Japanese, being island people, have a reverence for fish, the staple of their diet. They are also an extremely superstitious people, and they have a healthy horror of sharks. But the P-40's were later to carry another decoration which the Japanese like even less. For every Jap brought down, the victorious pilot is awarded a small Nipponese flag. This trophy, a bright red dot on a white background, is mounted just under the pilot's windscreen. Every one of the group has earned at least two of these awards; many have half a dozen. The late Squadron Leader Jack Newkirk had the side of his fighter lined with twenty-eight.

Because the Tiger is a favorite deity of the Chinese, the A.V.G. pilots called themselves Tiger Sharks. But they were Flying Tiger Sharks to the Chinese and became The Flying Tigers to the world.

Meanwhile, Chennault was preparing his main base at Kunming, deep in China's Yunnan hills. On the shores of a clear blue lake, six thousand feet above sea level, this station on the Burma Road was ideal for his purpose. Surrounding this base, he established an ingenious system of listening posts. First, "interceptors," Chinese volunteers, with little hand-powered portable radio transmitters, lie in wait off the Japanese airdromes. Then two circles, the first two hundred miles from his base, the second fifty miles nearer, are formed by other loyal Chinese—hundreds of them. Each is taught how to watch and listen for enemy aircraft, how to distinguish their types, measure their speed, determine their direction. In trials, the system was uncanny.

In November, Chennault reported to the generalissimo that A.V.G. was ready. He had only two full squadrons, one of ex-Army pilots, one from the Navy schools, and a flight group of eight made up of Marine-trained fliers. He had no reserves of either ammunition or fuel. But when war sped across the Pacific on that Sunday dawn of December 7th, Chennault's boys were ready.

On Sunday morning, December 21st, the first chance came. Six P-40's climbed into the clouds. Japan's first "invincible" squadron was shot to pieces. And six P-40's, without a scratch, came streaking home to Kunming—to report to "The Old Man."

Everything he had taught them had come true. After this first demonstration of the "Chennault System," there

32

was no curbing their enthusiasm. When the Japs attacked, their formation was just as he said it would be, they turned the way he said they would, they reacted just as he had sketched it for his pilots on the blackboard at Toungoo. Later, when Parker Dupuoy, of Seekonk, Massachusetts, hooked his wing into a Zero, he remembered what Chennault had said: "The Zero can outmaneuver and outclimb you. You are faster and stronger. These are your advantages. Use them." With supreme confidence in Chennault's teachings, the youngster pointed his nose into a dive—and watched the Jap's wing crumble like a piece of paper. From then on, "The Old Man" was regarded as infallible.

After four long years, Chennault was ready to deliver his first blow for China. But before he could strike, the British in Burma called for help: "Send the American Volunteer Group to Rangoon." When, just after dawn on the day before Christmas, only eighteen old-style P-40's swung into Mingalodon Airport at Rangoon, British faces fell. Eighteen planes! The R.A.F. had twice that number themselves. The alarm had already warned them that eighty Jap planes were even then on the way.

But neither the British nor the Japs figured Chennault into their totals—until the two forces met. The two British Squadrons returned with six Jap planes to their credit, with a loss of four of their own. The eighteen A.V.G. pilots came back with a record of nineteen Japs, their only casualty being a bullet hole through one wing of one of the P-40's!

Word of the spectacular victory swept like wildfire through China. In one lightning blow, the Japs' planned

33

blitzkrieg of Burma was thrown out of gear. That battle wrote the first line in an epic chapter of American courage which must forever stand as one of the brightest pages in her military history. Day after day, for sixty-two successive days, relays of Chennault's pilots met Japan's attackers head on.

The courage of this little band of American volunteers became the sparkplug of fierce Allied resistance all over the Asiatic mainland.

ESCAPE TO FREEDOM

By *Emile X*. By wireless from London[1]

This is the story of a one-time Belgian schoolteacher. It might have been the story of a Pole, or a Frenchman, or a Norwegian, or a Dutchman. For in the countries occupied by the Germans were many brave men to whom all the perils of a flight to England, where they might fight again, were small compared with the thought of living in slavery. From those who succeeded in reaching England new fighting units were re-formed. Some of these patriots have become Commandos, of whom you read elsewhere in this volume.

Before the outbreak of the war I was a school teacher in a small town in Flanders. My ambition was to lead a quiet life, to own my house, to dig in my garden, to play with my daughter after school hours. If any one had told me at that time that I would be arrested in three countries and that for the better part of eighteen months I would move about Europe in disguise, bearing forged papers, stealing food, cheating, lying, crossing frontier lines like a criminal, and that eventually I would row across the North Sea in an open boat, I would have smiled quietly and shaken my head. "No," I should have replied, "I am not the sort of man for that."

Yet despair makes adventurers of us all. A simple village school teacher, I traveled over 2,000 miles through

[1]From *The New York Times Magazine*, May 17, 1942, "A Story for Free Men," by Emile X. Copyright, 1942, by The New York Times Company.

Belgium, occupied France, Vichy territory, and Spain in search of a way to freedom, away from the reach of the Gestapo and the sound of tramping boots.

I was a soldier defending the Albert Canal when Hitler hurled his armies into my country. I retreated into France along with hundreds of other Belgian soldiers at the time that my King surrendered. We fought on from there, but after only a brief period we found ourselves surrounded near Calais.

I decided on a desperate gamble. The Germans were still a few miles away. I went to the nearest French farmhouse and got from the farmer a suit of civilian clothes and food enough to last for two days. Then I began my first game of hide-and-seek with the German Army.

I was determined to go home. I had to know whether my wife and children were still alive. Though I knew I could be shot without trial if I were captured, the urge to see my loved ones was stronger than my fear of death. For a week I traveled steadily by night, passing through the German lines, stealing a little food as I went along. By day I slept in the fields, hiding in the tall grass. Luck seemed to be with me. Every night I slowly crept a little nearer the Belgian frontier. My hopes were rising.

Then a blow came suddenly one night as I tiptoed through a village I believed to be empty of Germans. There was a shout of "Halt!" and before I could collect my wits I was brought before a German officer. He asked to see my papers. I had only my Belgian identity card. This bore the stamp of my regiment, a fact I had forgotten, or I should have destroyed it. I was placed in the guard-room to be dealt with in the morning.

All my hopes of escaping had now vanished. Gloom settled over me. But from the dark came the steady roar of approaching bombers, and with the whine of the first falling bomb confusion broke out in the village.

I heard the guards shouting and running, and the crash of masonry as one bomb hit. The British were raiding the place—but God was kind. I smashed the window in the rear of my prison room, crawled out, and made for the fields near by. I hardly noticed the bombs that continued to rain on the village. I was free once more.

How I reached my home town is no longer clear to me. I continued to live like an animal. I ate raw carrots, raw potatoes, and raw turnips when I could find any in the deserted fields I crossed. I spent one night in a brewery filled to the ceiling with German shells while British bombs dropped all around. I found an abandoned car and drove it until the gas gave out. I stole a bicycle and rode it until a tire burst. I crossed the frontier into Belgium without seeing a single German soldier on guard.

In my own country again, I breathed easier. Twice I stumbled into groups of German soldiers. But by this time I was such a scarecrow that they believed me when I said I was a civilian refugee returning home, and let me go. Once I even traveled on a German truck. The soldiers were being nice to my people.

After passing through Brussels, where an aunt of mine gave me food, a clean bed to sleep in and some fresh clothes, I again was on my way toward the coast. As I approached my home, I grew careless and was arrested for being out after curfew had sounded, but I managed to talk myself out of it. After more than three months I finally stumbled over the threshold of my little house.

It is not part of my story to describe my reunion with my family. My readers can well imagine it.

In a few weeks I was back at my old occupation of teaching. But life was now different from what it had been. Every family was in mourning. There was not enough food. The Germans had clamped down so many restrictions on what was to be taught in school and what was to be omitted that I began to think only of escape. I felt I could do my family better service by joining my countrymen in England. Here I could do little for them. In Britain at least I could fight for their freedom.

On visiting the coast not far from the town where I lived, I noticed a twelve-foot dory laid up on the sands. I wondered how I could steal it and get away. My friends in whom I confided laughed at me. They felt that it was not to be done, and in the end I agreed to forget about it. Yet the desire to get away grew stronger in me as my hatred for the Germans increased.

It was many months before I succeeded in establishing the proper contacts and became a member of one of the secret societies which, in spite of the greatest danger, managed to carry on right under the very eyes of the Nazis. I still carried on with my teaching, though by this time I had been "degraded" to the lowest class of the school because of "carelessness" in my history lessons. I had spoken of the last war. This subject was taboo, and the Germans had ordered all references to it cut out.

My school work was now only a cover for my other activities, and all this time I was planning my escape.

The day came, however, when my hand was forced. I was in Ghent when warning came that some of our men had been arrested by the Gestapo, that my own home was being watched, and that I must flee.

For three weeks I remained in hiding in a cellar in Brussels while my friends prepared a set of forged papers which were to permit me to travel openly across France and into Spain. Once in Spain I was to make my way to Lisbon or Gibraltar as best I could. These papers were so beautifully forged and bore such perfect copies of French, German, and Spanish visas that though my journey ended in failure they themselves were never questioned.

On my way through Occupied and Unoccupied France I met several other Belgians who, like me, were planning to escape via Spain. We traveled together, always stopping at certain addresses we had memorized before our departure. At these addresses were people who instructed us as to the best routes to take, warned us of the dangers ahead, and gave us food and money.

The blow came when we arrived at Carcassonne. There we learned of new regulations just issued by the Vichy government requiring a new stamp on passports of persons traveling into Spain. Our hearts sank as we debated what to do. In the end we decided to cross into Spain along a smugglers's route over the Pyrenees.

After one of the most grueling ten days of my life, I found myself back in a French prison cell. We had successfully crossed the mountain range—a terrible experience to those unused to climbing—when we were arrested by three Spanish carabineros [soldiers], who, after consulting an agent of the Gestapo, ordered us taken back to France.

There our money was taken, and we were sentenced to one month in jail for attempting to leave France without a proper visa.

Since our true identities had not been discovered, we still had a chance. After a month in jail we set out again, this time for Marseilles. There Robert, a former flier with the Belgian Air Force, joined me in trudging the water-front for three weeks trying to induce various ship captains to take us on as sailors, dishwashers—anything at all. Without seamen's papers it was hopeless.

Then through my despair I suddenly saw in my mind's eye a picture of that little dory beached on the sands of my country, seven hundred miles away. I knew then I must retrace my steps to make a final attempt for my freedom.

Robert insisted upon accompanying me, although I pointed out the dangers, and we began our long trek back on foot. Itinerant field workers in the French vineyards are entitled to food and rest on their employers' farms as a sort of advance against wages. Time after time we collected such advance payment, then moved on toward the north in the early dawn.

Crossing from Unoccupied France to Occupied France was the most dangerous part of our trip. This was accomplished with the help of a man who knew at least twenty good ways of getting across. Thus one night we found ourselves in a wood where our guide shook hands hastily and left us to go on alone. We crossed safely and in a few weeks were back in the cellar of the house in the Belgian capital, where our friends made new plans for our escape.

We had to adopt new names. I myself dropped my

40

own personality and became two other men with two separate sets of papers. All but natives were barred from the areas where I had to go, so I became a native of each area. Two different identification cards were forged for me. The first, which was to allow me to enter Bruges, bore a picture for which I had grown a mustache and worn glasses. For the second picture I had grown a beard. Somehow I managed to keep my dual personality without becoming mixed up and got to Bruges safely.

There I dug in for three weeks while I grew the beard I had shaved off to conform with my first identity. Then I set out for home, the vision of that small boat on the beach luring me on.

I passed through my home town late one night on my way to the coast, where I was to meet Robert. It was pouring rain, and I was thankful, for the rain helped conceal me from the German guards patrolling the town. I slunk from house to house and suddenly found myself opposite my own little home, where I knew my wife and children were. I crossed the street toward it and leaned against its walls. For a moment my determination wavered. Should I risk everything for a minute with my loved ones? From inside came the wail of my baby, born while I lay starving in a French cell. I yearned to see them. But I had fought far too long to give up now, and wearily I turned my back on my family and continued on my way toward the coast.

There I found Robert waiting for me at the house of a friend. The two of us were taken into hiding, where later we were joined by three others who were to make the trip across the North Sea with us. One was Jean, the former pilot of a tramp ship, the second Pierre, a sailor, and the third a young neighbor of mine, Hans.

While we stayed concealed in an empty villa [house], friends stole seventy liters of gasoline for us from the Germans, bought a small outboard motor, made a sail and mast, and saved up a little food and wine from their own meager rations. In a few weeks we were ready for our adventure.

We chose a dark, cloudy night, a Saturday. One by one we filed out toward the beach, passing close by three German sentries. We climbed down the breakwater onto the sand. Twenty yards away was another sentry. We hardly breathed, so quietly did we have to work. With a pair of shears we cut the line that held the dory to its mooring on the beach. The boat was one that was launched on wheels. These wheels were deep in the sand, and we had to lift up the whole thing and push. Every twenty minutes a German patrol passed, and we had to burrow into the sand and cover our noses and mouths with sand so that the dogs with the soldiers would not get our scent. We worked three hours before we could float the boat, afraid every minute that the moon would come through a break in the clouds and reveal us.

We had been rowing for two hours when the R.A.F. began a bombing raid on Zeebrugge. The crash of the bombs and the noise of the guns, we knew, would muffle the sound of our motor, so we started up. Jean, the former pilot, was skipper. He believed that we would reach England in another day or so. By dawn on Sunday our motor died, and we never were able to restart it. But we still had the sail and oars.

The breeze was blowing us toward England when a German bomber passed overhead. The bomber returned to circle us once, and soon four Messerschmitts appeared. They began to dive at us one by one as we lay trembling at the bottom of the boat. Machine-gun bullets spattered into our boat. Our captain was hit; the sailor, who jumped overboard, was killed instantly: Hans was severely wounded in the back; and my friend, Robert, had wounds in his head and right arm. Each plane returned four times, flying over us so low we could see the faces of the pilots. When they thought we were all dead they left us.

I was the only one who escaped without a scratch, though my suit was torn with bullet holes. I did what I could for the wounded with the few bandages we had, and stopped the holes in our dory with rags. Then I began to row. For four and a half days I kept it up until the flesh of my hands wore off.

My memory of what happened during the next five days is hazy and confused. Jean, our captain, the only one who knew how to navigate, died after terrible suffering, as did Hans. We buried them at sea. Robert and I were delirious part of the time. We managed, somehow, to keep awake by hitting one another on the chin. The cold was terrible, and we had nothing left to eat or drink. For three days we lived on a tube of mint-flavored toothpaste which we pretended was candy.

My hands hurt so much I had to grit my teeth to keep on rowing. Robert bailed mechanically as water kept pouring into the boat. I remember asking for a cup of hot coffee and listening to Robert describe an imaginary football game. All but one of our oars were swept overboard during a storm, and on Wednesday, our fourth day at sea, I rowed and steered with one oar.

We tried to cheer up one another, and swore to row and bail until we reached England. By Thursday morning our legs were frozen, and we could hardly move our hands. We fainted several times. At one moment in my delirium I started to step out of the boat, but my friend tripped me with the oar. I rowed all through Thursday night, hardly aware that I was still alive.

By Friday morning I could no longer go on. I was at the end of my strength. Robert and I shook hands. Let come what might, we could do no more. We both fell asleep knowing our end would come quickly. We never expected to wake up again.

I don't know how long we had been asleep when I heard the staccato rattle of machine-gun fire. Opening my eyes, I saw two speedboats firing at one another. Then one of them disappeared. I tore off my shirt, tied it to the oar and waved, all the while trying to shout. The remaining boat came toward us, its machine guns pointing at us. I wasn't sure whether it was German or British. I was past caring. It was over—the horrible ordeal ended. That's all I knew or cared.

It was a British boat. The crew swung their machine guns away from us and signaled "thumbs up!" The next thing I remember I was being carried ashore, rolled in a blanket like a sausage.

HOW O'HARE DOWNED FIVE
JAP PLANES IN ONE DAY

By *John Field*. By cable from Honolulu[1]

On February 20, 1942, a young Navy aviation lieutenant
from St. Louis made a name for himself. He shot down and
damaged more enemy planes in one day than any man previously, flying under any colors, is believed to have accomplished. A shy young man, Edward H. O'Hare, called "Butch"
for short, found it difficult to tell his story, and the first part of
it, as reported by Mr. Field, is therefore told by his squadron
commander, Lieutenant Commander John S. Thach, of For-
dyce, Arkansas.

Thach began the interview by presenting the background
of O'Hare's unforgettable flight, "Our carrier was operating in the southwest Pacific. We had hoped to surprise
the Japs but knew we might be spotted by patrol planes.
On the morning of February 20 we learned that such a
patrol plane was near us. To intercept this snooper I took
up my plane and another single-seater fighter. O'Hare
wanted to go, but I sent him back, figuring we'd need him
later. At a distance from the ship we entered a cloud and
bucked our way through a rainstorm. Far below was a
small opening and suddenly through the opening I saw
a huge Jap plane. It was a four-engined patrol bomber,
larger even than Pan American Clippers.

"I reported to the carrier immediately. I lost the big

[1]From *Life*, April 13, 1942. Copyright, 1942, Times, Inc.

bomber in the clouds. Desperately trying to find him again, I climbed above the clouds and dropped below them several times. At last I dimly saw a huge shape leaving the rain squall. I never lost him again. Back into the rain squall I went letting him get out into the open blue. When he was a mile out in the open blue, I started after him quickly. I overtook him with the other fighter protecting my tail, and I gained a position for attack.

"Suddenly, although I thought I was still out of range, he began shooting. I dove on him, let go with my guns and thought that I'd hit him as gas came out of his fuel tank. Then as quickly as possible I recovered and got set for a second attack. This time the wing man attacked with me, and we got him good. His whole upper wing, where the four engines are located, burst into flames. Suddenly he nosed over and his jettisoned bombs crashed into the water with a huge explosion. Neither the wing man nor I were hurt, but the wing man's plane had bullet holes. About twelve Japs, the entire crew of the bomber, were killed.

"On the way back to the carrier," Thach continued in the interview, "I heard that another snooper had been reported. He was intercepted at 6,000 feet, burst into flames, and crashed, killing the entire crew. We landed aboard the ship, ate a big lunch, and figured that we'd have more work before dark as we expected that before crashing the Jap patrol bombers had notified their shore bases of our presence. As a precaution we kept a division of six fighter planes in the air all the time.

"In the middle of the afternoon we had word that Jap bombers were coming. At that moment we had six planes in the air with six more which had just been relieved and were waiting to land. My planes were on deck waiting to go up. Then came nine Jap bombers, beautiful fast twin-engined jobs looking like B-26's. They came in three formations, three each at about 200 knots. Our planes, circling to land, got orders to go up and join the fight. We, too, got set. Then the fight started.

"The first time two of our fighters pressed their triggers two Jap bombers fell. Soon bombers were falling like flies all over the sky. As the Jap leader fell he tried to strafe the bridge of the U. S. carrier but failed. In seven to ten minutes of fighting all the Jap planes were driven away and most of them were destroyed. No bombs hit the water close to the carrier."

At this point O'Hare spoke up and described the next phase of the fighting. "Fifteen minutes later another group of twin-engined Jap bombers came on. This time we weren't quite as ready for them, since most of the fighters were being refueled and getting ammunition. Thach and another plane were off chasing what was left of the first Jap flight, and I was alone with one other plane over the ship.

"It soon developed that that plane, because of difficulty with the guns, was unable to fight so I was alone against nine Jap bombers.

"I first contacted them about twelve miles away from the ship," O'Hare went on. "They were flying fast and straight, straight for the carrier which they had apparently been ordered to get at all costs. Counting three machine guns and a cannon on each plane I figured I had to worry about twenty-seven different guns—not all at once, of

47

course. I got above them and prepared for the first group to pass. Quickly I dropped, pressed the trigger and saw two of them get hit and drop out. They burst into flames and fell. Actually, I figured, there wasn't much to do except shoot at them. I would go for one, let him have it, then pull out quick so that the exploding, burning plane would not fall on top of me. Then I'd go for the next one like the first.

"These bombers were coming in formations of three. On the first pass I hit planes on the right afterend. Then I went over to the left side and started up the line.

"In this way I shot down five and damaged one or two of the nine bombers. The last Jap I went after I could have downed except my gun stopped after ten rounds when I ran out of ammunition. My whole action took only three or four minutes. They tell me there were sometimes three falling planes in the air at once. I was still worried though because what Jap planes were left got through to the carrier.

"Fortunately other U. S. planes were now up in the air to give me support. They chased the Japs away, and though bombs dropped within 50 yards of the carrier, they did no damage. When the fight was over I thought I'd lost my voice. I screamed in the cockpit to see if my voice was O.K. It was. Only the transmitter had gone sour. By nighttime we had shot down eighteen of twenty Jap planes seen that day. One other was damaged and probably didn't get home."

DESERT BATTLE

By *Quentin Reynolds*. By radio from Cairo[1]

Somewhere in the African desert a burning sun looked down on a group of soldiers huddled in shallow trenches on a plateau. First came the German tanks and then later, in the light of a half-moon, came the Stukas. This story tells you how desert warfare looks, and feels, and sounds.

We had been surrounded on three sides; now word had come from our reconnaissance planes that fifty Hun tanks were coming from the fourth side to attack us. Finally in the distance we heard the unmistakeable quick, sharp bark of tank guns. They had opened fire with their seventy-fives at seven thousand yards. Soon the artillery supporting this division began to answer. Reports came to the general commanding every few minutes. He stood there with a six-day beard on his face and with his uniform in tatters, and there was something magnificent about his calmness. The reports were bad at first. Six British guns had been put out of action. The tanks were approaching closer to our plateau. They wanted it badly because it was a vantage point commanding this part of the desert. The general smiled when a grimy dispatch rider hopped off his motorcycle and blurted out, "We got seven of them." Seven of the big tanks lay burning in the desert less than

[1]From *Collier's*, January 3 and 10, 1942. Excerpts from "Desert Tank Battle," by Quentin Reynolds. Used with the permission of the author and *Collier's*. Copyright, 1942, The Crowell-Collier Publishing Company.

three miles away. Then he repeated the message in more military terms. But the others came on, and suddenly the general said casually, "There they are."

There they were. They were in single file, a departure from their usual attacking methods. Now they were only a mile away, and I counted twenty-three of them. They were for the most part the big Mark Four type, General Rommell's pets. Shells burst around them, sending up quick bursts of sand and smoke that hung in the still air. Sharp red flashes broke from the tanks, and lazy puffs of white smoke followed. We on the plateau were quiet and tense now. The guns from the other three sides began to throw shells at us, but we were too occupied in the amazing desert drama to hide in our trenches. Then one of the tanks received a direct hit. Its nose rose slightly in the air; it leaned drunkenly on its side; and then a column of black smoke spiraled up from it. The soldiers with me let out a yell. This might have been a football match with us as interested spectators.

Another tank was hit and still another, and now a pall of smoke hung over the battleground. The tanks were close to the borders of the mine fields surrounding our plateau. They tried to keep their single file, flanked by armored cars. There were five of them burning now, and the rest looked like bewildered beetles being attacked by some small vicious, unseen insect.

It lasted for one hour. I saw ten tanks go up in smoke, and then the Hun had had enough. The surviving tanks crawled away painfully, slowly, uncertainly. Some limped badly, and you knew that these were hurt. Their blunt noses swerved away from our plateau toward the west;

toward the protection of their guns, which were still shelling us viciously. Slowly the tanks merged with the horizon, and then they disappeared. And the shelling stopped, and a heavy exhausted quiet descended upon the desert, and we realized that we were limp with tiredness and with the burning heat of the sun. Official reports came in. The artillery had destroyed fifteen tanks within four hours—a nice morning's bag.

We slept well, but our awakening was rude. In my sleep I heard a steady buzzing, and it grew louder, and automatically I tried to brush away a mosquito that wasn't there, and then suddenly I was wide awake. The airplane was quite low. My watch said 4:45. The half moon gave little light to our battered plateau. The sky was a black curtain of velvet splashed with a million golden stars. I got out of my blanket, wondering idly whether this plane was one of "ours" or one of "theirs." We were not long in any doubt. There was a soft swish of something flying through the air, and then, high above, a burst of light blossomed to hang against the blackness, to light our small world. He dropped two more flares, one directly over us. He was like a surgeon preparing for a major operation. The flares were arranged methodically, and now our plateau was bathed in a penetrating white light. Flares sink very slowly and burn for five minutes. And now we knew that we were in for it.

For a minute or so the plane merely circled casually, and we huddled down in our very shallow trenches, waiting for it to come at us. We knew that we were in for a taste of the most horrible attack that modern warfare has as yet devised—dive bombing. I looked up and saw the plane, ghostly white in the light of the flares, standing distinctly against the black star-specked dome of the sky. It was just 5 A.M. And then I ducked quickly in the trench, for the noise of the motor had changed from a steady drone to a high, singing whine as the pilot leaned against his stick and pointed his airplane earthward.

The whine changed to a scream as the plane, loaded with death, hurled itself through the air. He was coming directly for our small patch of four short trenches. He dove to what seemed a hundred feet, and then came the bombs. They landed, and the world shook unsteadily, and the earth trembled, and the sides of my pitifully small trench dislodged sand and rock, and covered me with them, and the concussion threw me heavily against the side of the narrow trench, and a blast sent sharp flashes of pain through my head. And then he was gone. There was quiet, except for the drone of his motors above. There was the smell of smoke, and a new sound, a crackling noise. I stood up and saw that a large supply truck forty yards from my trench had received a direct hit. It was burning brightly.

I heard the plane returning and it was time to fall face downward in the loose sand at the bottom of the trench.

He was not alone this time. Word had gone out that there was good hunting to be had here on our plateau where a regiment of British soldiers lay hidden in the sand. They dropped more flares and circled casually, and the drone of the motors crept into your brain so that you wondered if the uneven hum would ever leave you. There were five of them. But now the Huns knew that we had no antiaircraft guns close enough to bother them, so they took their time. There was a minor explosion close by, and I stuck my head above the trench. I did that by merely sitting up. The fire had reached the gas tank of the supply truck, and the tank had exploded, a gentle explosion compared to the sound of the bombs.

Then, fantastically, the truck came to life. Roman candles shot from it in graceful curves. I could only think of the fireworks at the New York World's Fair. The truck unluckily had been full of flares and Very lights, and they cascaded beautifully from the wreck, blue and green, and white, and I could imagine the German pilots up there laughing, and talking to one another through their radios, saying, "Good joke, eh, Franz? The English shooting fireworks at us." And I was swept with a blind and quite illogical hatred of them. Hatred is a good, honest emotion, and it is useful, too, because when hatred grips you, fear leaves. And now they had decided to paste us again, and I flung myself in the trench and hated them.

All five of them dove at once. The bombs dropped all around my small trench, and time stood still, and nothing was real except the horrible sound of warfare at its worst.

They kept the bombing up for forty-five minutes that was an eternity. Then in the east a turquoise strip appeared on the horizon. It broadened and lightened to aquamarine and then the blue faded into a golden light, a merciful heralder of the dawn. But one more attack remained before the dawn banished these evil creatures of the night. This was perhaps the worst. When a plane dive-bombs, it cannot drop the very heavy bombs because it would itself be caught in the upward blast. These Hun planes had been dropping comparatively small hundred

53

pounders—small, perhaps, but each one quite capable of killing a hundred men. Now the planes flew high above us, and huddling there with our faces in the sand, we wondered what new deviltry they were hatching. Then came the screams of the big bombs they had been saving for last. These were the bombs I'd heard in London, a hundred times, and in Moscow, too. They sounded as though some celestial giant were tearing a piece of heavy silk; they sounded like the screaming of a thousand shrill-voiced, tortured demons, and then they landed. Again the world around us rocked, and the blast swept through the trench, and we embraced the earth of the trench without thinking, because by now our consciousness had been entirely dulled by the noise and the terror of it all. The world rocked, and then suddenly the dawn came to blast the darkness from the desert, and the desert was quiet except for the crackling of the flames from the burning trucks and the faint hum of the retreating Jerry planes.

NIGHT FLIGHT OVER ENGLAND

By *William W. White*. By telephone
from London[1]

How would it feel to meet a German bomber at night some-where over the English countryside? Or perhaps watch a German raid on an east-coast English town from 2000 feet in the air? Almost anything might happen up in the skies in the dark of the night. After weeks of waiting, the British Air Ministry granted Mr. White permission to go on a "non-operational" flight over England with an all-Canadian fighter squadron equipped with Bostons. What did happen you will read in the following story, which has a "surprise" ending.

The weather turned slightly "sour" close to take-off time, lessening our chances of spotting enemy aircraft, which are difficult enough to find even on cloudless, moonlit nights; but we took off anyway, at 1:32 A.M. The wing commander explained the "intruder" exercise he had planned—which meant going up the English Channel for fifty miles, then sweeping inland and "stooging" around a British airdrome and theoretically waiting to pounce on any "enemy" planes about to take off or land —was "almost as good as the real thing." That could only mean one thing—there might be a chance of bagging a real "Jerry."

But once in the air, skipping through alternate layers of wispy cloud, patches of bright moonlight and thick

[1]From *The New York Herald Tribune*, July 5, 1942. Copyright, 1942, New York Tribune, Inc.

mist, the story took on a different aspect. Through the intercommunications system the blond nineteen-year-old pilot called, "Look to your right! Looks like they're plastering Norwich!"

Sure enough, there it was—a raid witnessed from the best air-raid shelter in the world. Through the murky gray clouds, needle-thin, lightning-like fingers of burnished gold shot into the sky. "That's ack-ack (anti-aircraft fire)," the pilot yelled. Then rose-tinted flashes spread along the ground as bombs exploded. For almost the entire two hours and twelve minutes of the trip there was hardly a let-up. There was no noise, but anybody who had been in London during the blitz could dub in his own sound track.

The two of us, padded grotesquely with yellow "Mae-West" life-saving jackets and weighted down with parachute harness, gave up our role of spectators and became active participants when the voice in the earphones sharply reminded us, "Watch out for any Jerries. We'll have to get out of the way, since you guys haven't got any rear gun." Suddenly the fun of night-flying through enemy-infested skies lost its tang, and I wondered if any "Jerry" who came upon us would realize that this was strictly a "non-operational" flight.

The thought that planes are around you and that you might bump into one any second doesn't ease your tension. Then you remember you've forgotten to ask how to open your parachute hatch—and anyway, your parachute is lying somewhere on the floor and you can't bend down and get it, since you're packed into the gun turret as tightly as two fat men in a phone booth.

Keeping alive seems to become more complicated every second. The clouds, which a second ago formed a lovely, snow-white carpet underfoot, close in, choking out the half-daylight and plunging the plane into a dim mist, and you hear the observer beg the pilot to "try to find an opening."

The plane dives and you lose all desire to be an R.A.F. hero when you hear the pilot say, "This blankety-blank altimeter showed 200 feet, but I could have reached out and put a handful of water on that last dive. There's something wrong." Incidentally, the clouds were so thick we never found the "enemy airdrome."

The earphones clattered in a Chinese dialect, and the pilot said, "They're ordering us home. The weather's closing down." Then I asked, "How do you manage to get down at night with no ceiling?" "You'll find out—if we get down," he replied. I thought he was joking. He wasn't.

For the next two or three years or so it seemed, we cruised around, diving and climbing, trying to find an opening. One developed about three hundred feet from the ground near the station. A few minutes after we landed the rain came down in torrents, but we could still see the reflected flashes of German bombs and hear the sharp crack of anti-aircraft guns, so I still had a story—or thought I did until the commanding officer assured us there had been no Germans over England at all, that the ack-ack flashes were lightning (close) and the bomb flashes were lightning (not so close).

What we did not know until we landed was that the "Ops [Operations] Room" started calling us twenty minutes after we took off, trying to tell us to hurry home because it knew the weather was getting bad and was afraid we might have to circle around helplessly for hours or until the gasoline tanks went dry. It's just as well we didn't know.

RUSSIAN GIRL SNIPER

By *Lieutenant Lyudmila Pavlichenko*, Army of
the U.S.S.R.[1]

When Lyudmila Pavlichenko was in her teens, like thousands of other girls, she liked all kinds of athletics—running, jumping, discus-throwing, rowing, swimming. She was not interested in shooting until she heard a boy boast how good he was at it. Little did she think then that one day she would be fighting for her country and that for her bravery and marksmanship she would win some of the most prized Russian medals. This story of her life was written by Lieutenant Pavlichenko during a visit to the United States and Canada.

To begin with: I am a Ukrainian. I was born in the town of Belaya, Tserkov, not far from Kiev, twenty-six years ago. I am a most ordinary looking girl, medium height and with dark brown hair, which I used to wear long. I had to have it cut short as soon as war broke out, and now my cap covers it easily. For the rest, I have no particular distinguishing marks, except for a little scar on my forehead just above the bridge of my nose. That is a mark left by a German long-range shell splinter. I have four of these scars, by the way, but they don't bother me and didn't keep me very long in the hospital.

A few years ago I was invited to enter the Military Engineering School, but I wouldn't hear of it: least of all was I

[1]From the *Information Bulletin* of the Embassy of the Union of Soviet Socialist Republics, August 29, 1942. Used with the permission of the Embassy of the Union of Soviet Socialist Republics.

thinking then of war and military affairs. I was interested in history. In 1937 I entered Kiev University; I dreamt of becoming a scholar, instead of which, I have become a sniper.

I learned to shoot a long time ago, before I went to the university. It was purely accidental that I took it up. I was very keen on all kinds of athletics—running, jumping, discus-throwing, rowing, swimming, and I even thought of trying my hand at weight-lifting. The only thing I was indifferent to was shooting. Then I happened to hear a boy boast about how he had made eight out of ten points at a shooting range. I took a fancy to shooting at once—went in for it properly—and by 1938 I had gone through a snipers's school.

In the summer of 1941 I was in Odessa and fell ill just before the war. On June 15th I went into a sanatorium—on the 22d I came out. The war cured me at once of all my ailments.

They wouldn't take girls in the army, so I had to resort to all kinds of tricks to get in. And after a long time I did—I was a soldier like the rest—and took part in the defense of Odessa.

Let me tell you how I opened my personal account with the enemy; things like this aren't easily forgotten! My turn came to occupy the firing position. I lay there and watched the Rumanians digging themselves in only three or four hundred yards away. We were strictly forbidden by the commander to shoot without his permission. I passed the word down the line, "May I fire?" and waited impatiently for a reply. Instead the commander sent back the question, "Are you sure of hitting them?"

"Yes!" I said.

"Then fire!"

I got a grip on myself, forced myself to be steady and cool, took very careful aim—and fired! My Rumanian flung up his arms and dropped. I waited for a fraction of a second. Another head appeared over the top. I got that one, too. A third Rumanian cleared out.

Snipers' work is by no means easy. You go out while it is dark, at four or four-thirty, and come back late at night. You need great self-control, will-power, and endurance to lie fifteen hours at a stretch without moving. The slightest start may mean death. Though we snipers are hunters, we are also fair game for enemy snipers. Every step we take is under observation of enemy snipers —spotters. They try to mark our firing positions and keep them under machine-gun and artillery fire. That is why each of us has several firing positions—I am never more than two days at the same one—and you shoot only when you are quite sure of your aim, because every unnecessary shot gives away your position.

It was the German snipers who taught me caution, endurance, and restraint. If I so much as stirred a finger, a bullet would whistle just over my head, or at the back of my legs. Occasionally a German tin hat would appear, just a fraction of it, and you think, "I'll get that Fritz!" You fire and the tin hat waggles like the head of a toy elephant and disappears. It was only a German decoy to make the sniper betray his position. Following that, the Germans usually opened such a squall of fire that you dared not even raise your head. It was just terrible. From sheer fright you would call out, "machine gunners—save me!" Then the gunners would open fire—quiet the Germans down a bit—and you would be able to crawl back, more dead than alive, for a breathing space.

Of course that was only at the beginning. Afterwards I got used to the fire and the German tactics. I learned all their tricks, and how to keep my position a dead secret. After a while, things went very well.

We defended Odessa until October. Then orders came to evacuate. Evacuation was done in an exemplary manner. We took positively everything with us aboard ship. The airmen took their old wheels with them, and the cavalry even old horseshoes. So we went aboard and started for Sevastopol. Much has been written about Sevastopol. The history of wars can show nothing to compare with the defense of Sevastopol. We were one odd Russian to every ten Germans. One thousand and five hundred planes flew over the long-suffering town every day. The air shook with incessant cannonading, exploding shells and bombs. The sun was blotted out by clouds of dust and earth. We hadn't enough shells or food, but we hung on. The city had ceased to be—there was nothing save a heap of ruins—but still we hung on, battling from our stand on the ruins, shooting from behind every building, every elevation, or mound.

Not a clod of Sevastopol ground was given up without a fierce fight—not a step did we retreat without orders! We mowed down the Hitlerites like ripe grain. Drunk with blood as with vodka they swept headlong into the jaws of death. Fresh German divisions were driven in to take the place of those fallen—there was no end to them! The Germans had to pay a high price—too high—for the ruin that was once Sevastopol.

*Lieutenant Lyudmila Pavlichenko, outstanding Russian
girl sniper*

An early step in an R.A.F. raid—loading heavy bombs at a bomber station

Inside an R.A.F. Stirling bomber

Brigadier General James H. Doolittle, leader of the first air raid on Japan, receiving congratulations from President Roosevelt. Later General Doolittle was made commander of American air forces in Africa and became a Major General

Snipers were kept busy those days. We made things unpleasant for the Germans. They were terrified of us, and cursed us. No wonder—150 of our snipers had destroyed 1080 Fascists in twenty days! I myself trained 80 snipers during the war. Altogether they destroyed over 2000 Germans.

The Hitlerites did their utmost but wore themselves out trying to discover the whereabouts of our snipers and put them out of action. They spared neither men nor means on this. They would open sniper fire as during an offensive.

We found it very difficult to work. Every inch of ground was under fire—every bush or shrub that could afford cover for a sniper was marked down by the Germans. They not only knew our positions but they knew the snipers by name. I have heard them more than once shout through a loud-speaker, "Lyudmila Pavlichenko, come over to us. We will give you lots of chocolate and make you an officer." After a while they went into threats and you would hear the voice that had been so ingratiating bellow furiously, "You had better keep out of our way, Pavlichenko!" On my last day at the front they yelled, "If we catch you, we will tear you into 309 pieces and scatter them to the winds!" The figure "309" was the number of Fascists I had killed. They even knew that!

But they needn't have worried. Neither I nor any of our snipers had the slightest intention of falling into their clutches. My friend Nikolai Koval was caught in an ambush. Ten Germans surrounded him and told him to surrender. In reply, Koval flung a grenade, blew up himself and six Germans at the same time.

It seems to me that at the present time the principal task of every honest young man, regardless of his nationality, religious convictions and political views, is to exterminate the Hitlerites relentlessly. Everyone to whom his country's freedom, honor, and independence are dear, and who wants to save his family, should take to arms and fight the Fascists—fight them wherever he can—north or south, east or west, in the Don River steppes, or the plains of France, in the Norwegian fiords, or the Greek hills. He should not wait until the enemies come and seek him out, but he should go seek them out and destroy them! Every German killed is a step along the road to the liberation of mankind from Hitlerism.

HOW THE R.A.F. DOES IT

By *Russell Owen*[1]

"Last night a large force of bombers attacked targets in the Ruhr and Rhineland." Throughout the far-flung British Empire, in the United States, in Russia, in China, in South America, over the secret listening stations in France, Holland, Belgium, Czechoslovakia, Jugoslavia, Norway, Greece, and elsewhere, where those who loved freedom could still cheer in their hearts, such communiqués as this were greeted as steps forward in the hard march to victory. Back of each bombing raid lies an enormously complicated piece of planning, such as this story describes.

The pressure of warfare has produced in the air forces one of the most efficient weapons the world has ever seen. It is not merely a matter of flying a plane—this bombing business. It is not merely a matter of courage. It is a task of coordination, of constant watchfulness and observation, of photography, mechanical perfection, teamwork among the crew and among the ground forces, cool, calm judgment in the midst of hell.

Naturally, these bombing operations start at the top, in the office of the grand strategists, who decide what should be destroyed first and inform the commander in chief of the air force. He, in his underground, quiet chamber, decides what forces to use and the best way in which to

[1]From *The New York Times Magazine*, June 7, 1942. Used with the permission of the author and *The New York Times*. Copyright, 1942, The New York Times Company.

use them. Surrounded by maps and weather charts, with pins showing targets, and after consultations with his meteorological expert, he makes his plans. The number of planes from each group to be dispatched, their objective, and the number and type of bombs they will use are determined.

A group covers a large territory, and in it are many squadrons. The group commander, according to weather in his locality and the type and number of planes at his disposal, decides what squadrons to use. Then the orders go out to the stations, where the squadrons are dispersed.

When the orders reach station headquarters there takes place a lot of fast action. The bombs are trundled out on carriages and loaded in the planes, and a good "bombing-up" squad of twenty-eight men can load fifteen aircraft in two hours. The planes have been checked by mechanics and riggers, holes have been plugged, repairs made, electrical and oxygen systems inspected. The intercommunication telephone system comes in for special care, for through it the captain controls the operations of his crew and gets reports from them which affect his own tactics.

Then the crews, young men who have been sleeping or playing tennis or reading, doing what they please in an atmosphere most conducive to relaxation, go into what the British call the Briefing Room—a somewhat legalistic phrase—for their instructions. They are told what they have to do, what their target is, its importance, and the main features in every area that should be hit. If it is an oil plant they are told to hit the dehydrogenation plant, if possible, and to knock out the compressor house, which will create an explosion all its own. Lines of approach are indicated, although the final decision is left to the leader. And the instructions conclude,

"Get right up to your target and do your stuff."

Crews are told what enemy defensive action they may expect, whether from anti-aircraft fire or fighters, where the searchlights are, and the barrage balloons. They are told how to come back home, what weather they may expect when they arrive, and what the wireless frequencies are for the night. They don't use the wireless unless it is absolutely necessary for navigation. Dead reckoning and the stars—if the stars are out—are their main reliances, a fact which explains why bad weather so often checks bombing flights over Germany.

The time comes and they roar off, one after another, at intervals of a few minutes, to join formation later. Inside the planes it is dark. The navigator works under a pale amber light, as does the radio operator. The rear gunner sits alone out in the tail, detached from all the world, so that he can see the body of his plane only by turning sideways. This position bothers some men, to others it gives a sense of unreal and fascinating detachment. It is the rear gunner's job to watch for attacking craft from the rear; and it takes cold nerve to hold fire until it will be effective.

Dodging through the clouds, with wings gathering ice and propellers sometimes throwing it, windshields rimed at cold heights which often reach 35,000 feet where the temperature drops to 50 below zero, the bombers wing their way through anti-aircraft fire, beating off attacks, to their objective. Once there the navigator drops his parallel rules and his logarithms and tables of figures and crawls forward to the bomber's cockpit. On the larger American machines there is a regular bombardier—as we call him—as well as a navigator, and the navigator may man a machine gun if a mate is knocked out.

Then the bombardier guides the pilot over the target disregarding the shell bursts near by, and drops his huge bombs and incendiaries, either together or singly, as he wishes. When he has done his job, he calls to the pilot, "Bombs gone." A swift turn and climb, the gunners fighting off opposition, and the plane heads for home.

The stories of some of those trips are almost beyond belief. Pilots shot, crews unconscious from altitude because oxygen pipes were broken, parts of the planes shot away or on fire, landing gear carried away—and yet many get home even from such flights, and are guided down the flare-lighted path to a desperate landing.

The watchers on the operations towers heave a sigh, and wait for the next plane.

FIRST CALL ON TOKYO

By *Brigadier General James Harold Doolittle*

At 12.30, Saturday, April 18, 1942, in full daylight a fleet of United States bombers swept in from the sea. For the first time in 2602 years Japan was subjected to enemy assault on its island cities. This was the answer to the cry that had come from millions of Americans immediately after December 7. Realistic people, however, scanning their war maps saw that Tokyo was 3850 miles from Pearl Harbor, 2460 miles from Dutch Harbor, 2419 miles from Midway (which had no bombers for such a task), 5131 miles from San Francisco. Only Vladivostock was close at hand, but Russia and Japan were at peace. Laughingly President Roosevelt said that the planes came from Shangri-La —from nowhere. Almost a month later it was revealed that the leader of the seventy-nine volunteers in the twin-motored B-25's which made the attack was none other than the famous "Jimmy" Doolittle, an aeronautical engineer and one of the world's greatest speed flyers. His aviation career began as an aviator in the United States forces in the First World War. As a professional soldier he was the first to take off, fly, and land by instruments. He set distance records and tested wings and engines. Once on a mission to a South American country to sell planes for an American company he learned that a German aviation ace had showed up at the same place on a similar mission for a German aviation company. Doolittle was in the hospital with two broken ankles, his feet in plaster casts. Hearing that the German was to give a demonstration, Doolittle ordered his plane warmed up and went into the air despite the plaster casts and his doctor's protests. He outstunted the German, won a dog-fight exhibition, got on the German's tail, and "flew" him down to the ground. The South Americans cheered. On July 1, 1940, Doolittle re-entered the Army Air Corps. On the day of Pearl Harbor he told friends, "I'm going to get in this thing with both feet. I'm going to Tokyo with a load of bombs." General Doolittle's statement of the bombing was released at the White House, where he went to receive the Congressional Medal of Honor from President Roosevelt. All the volunteers who accompanied him were nominated for the Distinguished Service Cross. Where the planes came from and where they went remained, for the time being, a secret.

The success of the recent air raid on Japan exceeded our most optimistic expectations. Each plane was assigned specific targets and the bombardiers carried out their expert duties with admirable precision.

Since the raid was made in fair weather in the middle of the day and from a very low altitude, no trouble whatever was experienced in finding the exact target designated. Apparently there was no advance warning of the raid, as we experienced little hostile reaction. Not more than thirty Japanese pursuit planes were observed during the flight and they were completely ineffective. Several we know were shot down, possibly more. Incidentally, the pilots of these planes seemed somewhat inexperienced, evidently not up to the standard of those encountered in active theatres.

We approached our objectives just over the housetops, but bombed at 1500 feet. The target for one plane was a portion of the navy yard south of Tokyo, in reaching which it had passed over what apparently was a flying school, as there were a number of planes in the air. One salvo made a direct hit on a new cruiser or battleship under construction. They left it in flames.

After releasing our bombs we dived again to the tree-tops and went to the coast at that altitude to avoid anti-aircraft fire.

Along the coast line we observed several squadrons of destroyers and some cruisers and battleships. About twenty-five or thirty miles to sea the rear gunners reported seeing columns of smoke rising thousands of feet in the air.

One of our bombardiers strewed incendiary bombs along a quarter of a mile of aircraft factory near Nogoya. Another illuminated a tank farm. However, flying at such low altitudes made it very difficult to observe the result following the impact of the bombs.

We could see the strike, but our field of vision was greatly restricted by the speed of the plane and the low altitude at which we were flying. Even so, one of our party observed a ball game in progress. The players and spectators did not start their run for cover until just as the field passed out of sight.

Pilots, bombardiers and all members of the crew performed their duties with great calmness and remarkable precision. It appeared to us that practically every bomb reached the target for which it was intended. We would like to have tarried and watched the later developments of fire and explosion, but even so we were fortunate to receive a fairly detailed report from the excited Japanese radio broadcasts. It took them several hours to calm down to deception and accusation.

The citation for the Congressional Medal of Honor which General Doolittle received was read by General George C.

Marshall, chief of staff of the United States Army, at the White House presentation ceremony:

"Brigadier General James H. Doolittle, United States Army, for conspicuous leadership above and beyond the call of duty, involving personal valor and intrepidity at an extreme hazard of life. With the apparent certainty of being forced to land in enemy territory or to perish at sea, General Doolittle personally led a squadron of Army bombers, manned by volunteer crews, in a highly destructive raid on the Japanese mainland."

THE FIGHTING–EST OUTFIT
IN THE BRITISH ARMY—THE COMMANDOS

By *J. Wilson McCutchan*[1]

Noisy little gunboats blast at Nazi pillboxes. Men creep ashore and blow up pumping stations, bridges, and buildings. Overhead bombers roar and pound. The Commandos are at it again. Organized and first commanded by Admiral Sir Roger Keyes, hero of Zeebrugge (some credit General Sir Archibald Wavell with the first idea), the Commandos have established a magnificent name for themselves and have won enough battle honors to rival any old-line regiment in the British Empire. This story tells what it takes to be a Commando and of some of their activities in Africa.

The Commandos bob up in France, wreck a strategic dock or power plant, grab a few prisoners, vanish. They make a dark-night foray on the coast of France or Norway. They harass an Axis outpost in Libya.

Commandos are the super-guerillas, the modern Apaches of the British Army. They are a tough, hard-trained, ruthless hit-and-run corps, the pick of the daredevils of the modern armies. They spread apprehension, disorganization, confusion, destruction, terror, wherever they land.

The name Commando goes back to South Africa, where it was applied to quasi-military expeditions sent by

[1]From *The New York Times Magazine,* April 5, 1942, "Hard-Hitting Commandos," under the pen name of Peter Locke. Used with the permission of the author and *The New York Times.* Copyright, 1942, The New York Times Company.

the Boers against the natives. Later it was used when those same Boers put some very efficient and destructive bands of organized guerillas in the field and gave the English nasty wallops that have been remembered for forty-odd years. There's a man in the British War Cabinet who has vivid memories of South Africa and the Boer War. His name is Winston Churchill.

For operational purposes the regiment has established battalions of flexible size at different points. Oldest in point of service are the English, Scottish, and Middle East Commandos. More recent are the Canadian, Indian, and Australian units. The names, except for the Canadian and Australian groups, indicate zones of activity rather than origin of personnel. All are off-shoots of the original unit, members of which assist in the training of the new men. Like the amoeba they are self-propagating. Most obvious advantage of their organization is this flexibility of command and movement. Red tape is reduced to a minimum and Commandos have disproved the adage that one can be in only one place at a time.

Appointment to the Commandos is limited to men who have done at least eighteen months with a regular infantry, cavalry, or artillery regiment. It promises a man no promotion in rank, no mention in dispatches, no decorations, and the nerviest, most daredevil jobs going. There is no extra pay for additional risks.

Every man who seeks a transfer to the Commandos must get the personal recommendation of his former colonel, together with his approval of the change, and, in theory, he must be unmarried and without dependents back home. Commando service is thus purely voluntary, for officers and men alike, but so many applications are received that the ranks might be filled three times over.

One group of one hundred and twenty men with whom I spent some two weeks on a troopship could muster men who had been in the Royal Irish Fusiliers, Royal Horse Guards (Household Cavalry), Durham Light Infantry, Northumberland Fusiliers, Twenty-first Lancers, and others. The sergeant major was from the Cameron Highlanders, and a second lieutenant from the Black Watch. There were a Norwegian and two Americans. Like their comrades, they had transferred from other British units.

English, Scotch, Irish, American, they are alike in two things: supreme confidence in self and in the regiment and an overwhelming desire to get at Jerry. Most of them are big men who can think and move quickly. A few are small and wiry, quite capable of taking care of themselves. All are in first-class physical condition and keep that way. They don't have a chance to get muscle-bound, and none would pass for "Sweethearts on Parade." All have a far-away look in eyes of steel that seldom twinkle. The twinkle will come again after the war.

Probably the biggest difference between the Commandos and the ordinary British regiment is the spirit of democracy which runs through all ranks. You don't high hat the man who may come up behind you just when you need him most. It isn't easy in the dark to keep a husky German sentry from letting out a yell that will set the whole camp loose and ruin everything.

On duty or off the Commando is the best disciplined, most orderly man in the empire armies. A Commando man will never let his job in hand or what's ahead get him down. Worry isn't his business. That's for the commanders. The order's the thing. Every man goes all out to reach the objective, at the same time giving perfect teamwork to his fellows. Some of them have played on the grounds of Eton and Harrow. The result counts.

Training of these picked men is highly specialized. It differs according to the arena of the war and the climate and topography in which they are likely to be engaged. Swimming noiselessly with full equipment, including pack and rifle, may be highly useful to an English Commando, but it doesn't help his brother in the Middle or Far East very much. To him desert or jungle sense and toughness are more important.

Six months is the average time necessary to train a Commando. In Egypt, where I knew them best, work in the desert naturally plays a large part. After practicing field tactics and reconnaissance for twelve hours under a summer sun in the Suez Canal Zone one company on emergency rations and without water did a forced march of thirty miles across loose sand between 5 P.M. and midnight. That's good tramping in anybody's army.

Jiu-jitsu is another feature of their program. They call it "unarmed personal combat." A little catch-as-catch-can and free-for-all fighting are thrown in for good measure. No holds or blows are barred. One man told me, "I spent two weeks in bed because I got fresh with the instructor. Thought I knew as much as he did."

There is a special course in grips and death locks peculiarly suited to enemy uniforms. Were German and Italian sentries not required to wear certain parts of the regulation equipment at night, they might be alive today.

All this training is hard to take. Many never complete it but are sent back to their old regiments. Those who make the grade limp about with bruises and sprains. There's only one proper way to learn how to break a choke hold on your neck. They don't have time to brush away the rocks, and they don't use mats to practise on either.

When a man does finish he may feel like a movie star coming out of a pro football game, but he has unlimited confidence in his own personal ability to meet whatever the dark night may offer.

One of the hardest tests is night stalking and patrol, a sergeant from the Royal Horse Guards explained. "They string up fifty yards of wire, about ten yards deep and fastened to regulation steel posts. Then at either end they post sentinels, usually from a rival platoon in your own company. Your job is to get through that wire without being caught.

"You've got a three-hour period in which to make the trial. There are no battle or camp noises to help you and every pebble you kick up sounds like a landslide. Those chaps on guard don't sleep the way the Eye-ties (Italians) do, either. Good practice though, and these help a lot." He held up a foot for inspection.

The shoe uppers looked like any ordinary high-top army boot of heavy pliable leather. The soles were thick, soft rubber. A Commando's working clothes are as adaptable as the man himself; this isn't a dress-up war. Charcoal and soot off the frying pan help to deaden the highlights of face, hands, and metal. Last-minute changes to suit a situation are necessary, and the trooper is skilful at using available cover and shadows.

All the Middle East Commandos saw action in Libya and Ethiopia. Cairo seethed with rumors of strange and terrible happenings to the Italians and Germans. Italian dispatch riders dashed up to headquarters' tents to find senior officers lying with throats cut open. Maps and orders thrown upon the ground. Sentries dead on the sand without a mark on them. The effect on Axis morale was tremendous. And all the while never any mention in reports or communiqués of Tommy who was doing the work. Nobody worried about that part of it, though. These young men enlisted for effect, not for glory.

Several Commandos got their initiation into real battle in East Africa. General Cunningham needed some trouble shooters and sent for them.

Gallabat is listed as one of the British victories of that campaign, but part of the Empire Army would gladly forget what happened there. What English newspapers call "a well-known county regiment" and which we'll call the Chiltshires for convenience, did "a bit of a funk." The Italians sent over some smoke shells one afternoon. Somebody shouted, "Gas! Gas!"

Normally the Chiltshires carried their gas masks, but somehow on this day they had left them back at the ordnance dump. Almost to a man the Chiltshires pulled their stakes and left the field to the Italian artillery, who couldn't understand why smoke shells should succeed where high explosives had failed.

What saved the day, but made it worse for the poor Chiltshires, was that two of His Majesty's Loyal Indian regiments were holding up the flanks. The Indians lowered their bayonets, charged through the smoke, and carried

British Commandos attack under cover of a smoke screen

Tough training makes Commandos and Rangers superlative
fighting outfits

General Douglas MacArthur, a born soldier whose heroic defense of the Philippines will be long remembered

A Filipino soldier of the 1st Filipino Infantry Battalion training in the United States practises throwing a hand grenade. This battalion will give Filipinos a chance to fight for the restoration of their homeland and avenge Bataan

the positions, but the white man's prestige was gone. No longer were the English pukka sahibs [Honorable Sirs]!

The colonel got the sack along with some junior officers of that regiment, but that didn't help the Indians' opinion any. Something had to be done, and that's where the Commandos enter. Just what they did was not fully told, but it was mighty. A rangy, sun-blackened kid from Oxfordshire summed it up: "There were only fifty of us. My first experience under enemy fire. Our objective was the key to the whole battle. I'll never forget those machine-gun bullets clipping the grass three inches above my head. There were things on the ground, too. Patrols had been out the day before and not all of them had got back. Somehow we got there and did the job. Forty-five of us got through. We were lucky that time.

"Next day we got our satisfaction. An Indian non-com met a couple of us on our way to the canteen. 'Pukka sahib,' he said, 'if there were just one hundred and eighty of you we could run these Italians out of this land to-morrow.' That meant more than any citation in dispatches."

No mention of the Commandos is complete without a word for Fanny. Fanny is the badge of the regiment when her miniature is pinned on the big "digger" hat (a large, wide-brimmed, campaign hat, cocked on one side and dating back to the time of King Charles), and she's the last resort when carried on the hip. Imagine a seven-inch curved blade with a knuckle-duster for a handle. That's Fanny.

Taken from either end, Fanny is altogether the most destructive looking weapon ever issued for hand-to-hand fighting. She and her miniature sister on the hat were designed specially for the Commandos. A trooper feels lost without her, though the chances are that he will seldom need her.

A serious young private told me: "She's not meant to cut with. The blade isn't awfully sharp, better for gouging and ripping. The brass knuckles are the most useful part of her."

He looked a little sad and added: "In fact, we're advised to wait and use the blade chiefly when the fighting's over. Leaves horrible marks, quite terrifying to whoever happens to find the poor fellow first. Sometimes we leave Fanny too—just to throw a little fear in the right place."

NIGHTS WITH A NIGHT FIGHTER

By *John R. D. Braham*, *D.F.C.*, Squadron Leader,
R.A.F. By wireless from London[1]

One of the most hazardous wartime flying jobs is that of the
night fighter. He hunts in the dark with German planes as his
prey. Squadron Leader Braham, who is in his early twenties,
is one of Britain's night-fighter aces, with nine enemy planes to
his credit at the time this story was written. Before the war he
was a post-office clerk in a hamlet near Cambridge, England,
where his father—an R.A.F. pilot in the last war—is a minister.

Our squadron was one of the first to be organized almost
three years ago, just after the war started. Night-fighting
was an undeveloped art at that time. We had to go up
night after night in Blenheims against an enemy who outnumbered us five, and often ten, to one.

On those early nights the partly trained Royal Observer
Corps, inadequate searchlights, and sheer instinct were all
we had to guide us toward the unseen enemy. Most of
the time we spent miserable hours in all weathers stooging
in darkness—"stooging," if you haven't heard, is the night-
fighter's term for a patrol which even today is a bit of a
bore. During the first few months of the service ground
observers seldom got us nearer than within five miles of
our prey. We would pick up from that point and grope
our way toward him.

[1]From *The New York Times Magazine*, September 13, 1942.
Used with the permission of the author and *The New York Times*.
Copyright, 1942, The New York Times Company.

It was not until a few of us got at the Huns that night-fighting got into our blood. It becomes a kind of fever that a man cannot shake off, once the virus seizes him. Anyway, with superb Beaufighters and a vastly improved spotting and guiding system, we can look back on it all and see the extraordinary development that has taken place since we first ventured into the night skies. Our bags have increased enormously. I, for one, wouldn't change for anything.

I got my first Hun one night in August, 1940, somewhere over the Hull district on the East Coast. Searchlights picked him out for me, and I was so excited that I opened fire long before he entered my gun range. My gunner did for him. We saw his plane change into smoke and flame, followed him down, and watched him crash on the beach. I had been "browned off"—"burned up" is the American expression, I think—with profitless stooging over cities which the Hun had burned and bombed. But this was my dish. All our lads felt the same when we began to get a few of their pack.

Actually we are little or no different from our lads in the day-fighters and day-bombers. It is not true, for example, that we have a cat's eye, or that we swallow incredible amounts of carrots to improve our night vision. Our diet is like that of any other flier, though we do get liberal doses of halibut liver oil pills. They make up for the time we lose out of sunlight—we sleep a good part of the day—and they act as a sort of tonic to keep us generally fit.

It is true that many lads among the day-fighters never make night-fighters. This is because their vision is slightly less sharp than ours. Most of our men, as a matter of fact, are former day-fighters and day-bombers. On the average our men are a little older than the crews on day operation.

Experience is the prime factor, of course. A man doesn't really get the hang of things under six months of night flying. About that time a lad begins to think he has got his business "buttoned up," as we put it. This is especially true if he has bagged a Hun or two, and some lads do have rotten luck. We have good men in our squadron who have two hundred hours of night stooging to their credit, but just never had the good fortune to meet up with Jerry.

On the other hand, some of our chaps have had the rare good luck to shoot down a Hun the first time out. That is almost like pricking your finger on a needle in a haystack with the first jab in the dark. It doesn't happen often. It takes time and patience—indeed, you rather develop a sort of nose for it and become a nocturnal pointer, as it were.

It is probably difficult to understand until you have done it, but it is not long before a new night-fighter learns to see the enemy on the darkest nights and in the dirtiest weather. You learn to look for tiny reddish spots of flame from the exhaust of the Hun's motors. You spot them more quickly on dark nights than you do on clear nights. When stars are sharp and brilliant or when there is a flood of moonlight, the exhaust flame pales and is harder to pick out.

After a little while on the darkest night and from the highest altitudes you can pick out where the land or the shore ends, where the sea or the channel begins. It appears to the practiced eye as if it were put in with a pencil.

At first enemy ships get by you and vanish before you know, but later you learn to pick out the telltale exhaust and quickly distinguish the tiny, vague, black thing that is your target. The trick then is to close in fast, get on his tail at gun-range, and let him have it.

Clear nights are better, though, in one way. You needn't keep your eyes forever changing focus from searching the heavens one minute and, the next minute, scanning the luminous dials on your dashboard. You spot horizons quickly and can even read landmarks—roads and railways, for instance—thousands of feet below, as you would read a good map under a bright lamp. Then you always know where you are, and it is easier on your eyes.

We scrambled out one night on a quick call and—this answers the tosh about cat's eyes—I tripped over a starting battery lying on the field and jolly near broke my neck. It was the night I got my second Hun—a Dornier 215.

We ran across him 12,000 feet up. It was cold in the early Beaufighters—we had no heating. The oil had frozen in the breach locks of my cannon, and when I pressed the firing button, the guns were dead. We chased the Hun a distance before my observer got the breach locks cleared and ready for action again.

We must have been within one hundred yards of Jerry's tail when I got in the bursts. He literally blew up. Great chunks of the flaming Hun plane flew back at us and the explosion rocked us.

Though I live forever, I shall never forget Coventry, Birmingham, and Liverpool. How they filled my heart with a hatred I had never known before—hatred for creatures who would war that way on helpless women and children!

Certainly I shall never shut out the picture of burning London. When I took off from our airdrome that night, I saw the glow of London's fires even before I had lifted the wheels from the runway. From the night sky that fire was a fearsome spectacle—as if hell had broken loose on earth.

As I flew toward London at 12,000 feet up I saw two Heinkels about one hundred yards apart in a twin formation. I went for the nearest—lefthand one. I guess we fought five minutes, and that is a long fight as night-fighting is counted.

I got in some close bursts but didn't seem to have him quite right. I could see white sparks chip off his ship but no killing hit. Finally he dived cloudward and I followed, and he let me have a taste of his stuff. When you are in flight, you hear nothing but your own motors and what comes in over your "R.T."—radio telephone—but at that moment I heard a sound as if some one was hammering sharply on my fuselage.

I had never heard that sound before. I got in another squirt and put the port engine of the Heinkel out of action. He went into a crazy spiral and—so I heard later—crashed on Wimbledon Common. The other Heinkel cleared off, though why he didn't pick me off, I have always wondered.

When I got back to the airdrome late that night, I figured out who had been hammering my fuselage. It was that Heinkel I finally dropped. He had put about six of his best into my wings fuselage. It was the first time that any of my ships had been winged.

When a night-fighter has put in a number of hours he gets "rest"—that is, he is sent to spend six months in

85

training of new kids in the business. I ran into a marvelous bit of luck during one of those periods. I had a two-day break from this operational training, and I had come back in the evening to visit the squadron when word came through that the Huns were over Canterbury.

I asked the commanding officer if he would be good enough to lend me a Beaufighter and, much to my delight, much to the disgust of the chap whose ship I got—I got another Hun. He had bombed Canterbury and was streaking homeward, and his crew were probably figuring what they would have for breakfast. I had 340 miles per hour on my air-speed indicator when I caught up with them. I got in a squirt of 250 yards, and his fuselage caught fire. He blew up—a big chap—that is a Dornier-100. He went down into the sea—one last splash of flame.

Between operations we lie around the operations hut and usually have a bit of small talk. If you are next out— that is on "readiness duty"—you wear your Mae West flying kit and boots. That is in order that you may lose no time getting off. When the fellow turns from the phone and says, "Next out," and gives the enemy altitude and course, you tear off immediately. When you are up, R.T. keeps you in touch with the enemy's progress and brings you fairly close to that point where your eyes take over.

There is a certain beauty that night-fighters come to know which day-fighters and the earthbounds shall never cast eyes upon. The night-fighter, for example, often leaves the ground at dusk when the earth is hazed, darkened, and clouded in. He ascends 15,000 to 20,000 feet where he catches up with the sunset.

You don't see such sunsets from the earth—not the same reds, orange and gold as you see spread on clouds thousands of feet below. It is often the same when you are up before dawn stooging through the sky. Your eyes see extraordinary yellow light effects on the clouds an hour or two before the earthbounds sight the morning sun.

Not that you have much time for that sort of thing. The pilot who is dreamy and poetic and doesn't keep his mind on his business, won't live long at night-fighting.

I would like to get in a word for the chaps who never get any credit—certainly not the credit they deserve. I mean our ground crews. They make our night fighting possible. Without their sweating at our ships and keeping them absolutely tuned, we would never get full efficiency out of our planes. They are a great lot of lads who work on with no thought of special honor and glory.

WAR COMES TO THE PHILIPPINES

By *Lieutenant Tom Gerrity*, United States Air Corps[1]

December 7, 1941, is a day that will live forever in American history. In the cities, in the towns, in the peaceful countryside Americans were stunned, alarmed, angered. On December 7 to many in the United States an immediate attack upon the Pacific coast was a grim possibility, in spite of thousands of miles of ocean. What of the Philippines, which lay directly in the path of the aggressor? Lieutenant Tom Gerrity of the United States Air Corps kept a record of those first days and of all the heroic days that were to follow. He wrote in pencil in a dime-store notebook and doubtless never dreamed that his words would be read. The first entry was written at Fort McKinley on the day the war broke out, December 8, west of the International Date Line. Before the fall of Corregidor, Lieutenant Gerrity was flown to Australia. At the time this book was prepared, he held the rank of major.

December 8. We were awakened by news that Hawaii has been attacked. A state of war exists between the United States and Japan. The story seems almost unbelievable. To have the Japs make a successful attack on one of our strongest fortresses.

Our group is on the alert. We wear gas masks, steel hats, and pistols. Major John Davies has assigned some of us to fly B-18's [medium bombers] on bombardment missions.

[1]From *The Chicago Times*, "Bataan Diary," by Lieutenant Tom Gerrity. Copyright, 1942, Chicago Times, Inc.

At 9 A.M. we hear Ibas had been attacked and many pursuit planes destroyed [Ibas is an airdrome 150 miles northwest of Manila]. Clark Field was hit, many Fortresses and P-40's were destroyed on the ground. Casualties were heavy.

We had three air raid alarms tonight. I wasn't impressed and tried to turn over and get some sleep but there was too much excitement around me. On the last alarm the Japs did come over, bombing Nichols Field from about 1500 feet.

Overanxious Philippine troops fired 30-caliber machine guns at them. It was a pretty sight to see their tracers cutting through the night like roman candles—but a useless display.

December 9. Still waiting for planes from America and hoping—been waiting since the 20th. There are often rumors that planes are at the dock. Once we even sent crews to the dock to assemble them.

Many flares are being sent up tonight—we suspect much Fifth Column activity all around Manila. We can see the flares—that's about all that can be done about it. It's impossible to hunt them down in the blackout.

December 10. I was ordered this morning to take a bomb load from Nichols Field to bomb the Jap ships in Lingayen Bay. We have three B-18's. Gus Heiss of Houston, Texas, Frank P. ("Pete") Bender of Brooklyn, and I piloted them. We loaded the bombers, then got orders to take off south because a Jap raid was supposedly due.

I couldn't start my right engine and our plane was left

behind. I went to the post command and received instructions to stand by because some other B-18's were returning. I returned to the ship at 11.30 A.M. We worked to get the ship in commission.

Without any warning the Japs came in with Zeros—at least fifteen of them. Everyone but the crew chief and I got under cover. We stood in front of the plane's nose while the Japs strafed.

I felt a stinging blow on the back of my left hand, looked down, and noticed it was bleeding. The B-18 was hit many times by explosive shells. Gas was running from the wing tanks into the bomb bay doors which were open, so I could see the demolition bombs hanging from the racks.

The Nips apparently swerved toward my ship because it was silver—it hadn't been camouflaged. After the 15th Zero had strafed us we saw our chance to run to a dirt pile about fifty feet away.

I figured then, "If the Japs don't get me now, they never will." We crawled under a mattress we found there just in time. A minute later our plane exploded, throwing fire all over us.

We jumped up immediately and ran around the corner of the dirt pile to beat the flames. Then bombs from the burning plane exploded, raining dirt and debris.

By this time I was wringing wet and scared to death. I lost contact with the crew chief but ran on to Sergeant Eugene Day, another crew chief, who was hiding behind a dirt pile, and he joined me under the mattress.

He turned up a corner of the mattress to take a look and was clipped across the bridge of the nose with a shrapnel splinter.

Then the Jap bombers came over. There were two waves. We could hear them, but we were afraid to look. When the bombs came, they dropped as close as fifty feet away. A few minutes later things began to quiet down. I decided to take Day to the post command for first aid. We were both weak from the shock of bomb explosions and still scared to death. The rest of my crew was O.K. I picked them up in a truck and drove to Fort McKinley while the doctor patched up Day.

December 11. Many Air Corps men from Clark and Nichols Fields are in the hospital with me. They have interesting stories to tell. We had an air raid alarm Wednesday night. All patients who could walk gathered in the courtyard downstairs. These Manila sirens are more alarming than the Jap bombers.

A BORN SOLDIER

By *Tom Wolf*[1]

This story is somewhat different from the others in this book. It is not strictly a war experience or achievement but rather a thumbnail sketch of the man whose life has been all "war" experience and achievement. To many Douglas Mac-Arthur symbolizes the true fighting spirit.

To a watching world, General Douglas MacArthur's long defense of Bataan seemed a military miracle. To those who knew his long career, it was just MacArthur—the same MacArthur whose record was an army legend even before the Japs swooped down on Luzon.

The General's life story reads like a "Tom Swift in the Army," full of bests, firsts, mosts, and onlys. An army man, from the day he was born, he has, in his sixty-two years, heard the zing of Indian arrows, the crash of Mexican rifles, the thunder of artillery on the Western front, and now the explosion of Japanese bombs. His valor and distinguished services have won him more American decorations—13—than were ever accorded any officer, and medals from ten foreign nations besides.

MacArthur graduated from West Point at the head of his class in 1903, with the highest scholastic record in twenty-five years. At thirty-eight he was the youngest

[1]From *The Cleveland Press* as condensed in *The Reader's Digest*, April, 1942. Excerpts from "MacArthur on Bataan," by Tom Wolf. Used with the permission of *The Cleveland Press* and *The Reader's Digest*. Copyright, 1942, by the publishers.

division commander in the A.E.F. At forty he was the youngest commandant ever to run West Point. He became Chief of Staff at fifty, the youngest full general in American history.

His first recollection was the martial sound of bugles at the barracks in Little Rock, Arkansas, where he was born in 1880. His first childhood trip was with the army, to his father's new post in New Mexico. There, when he was four, he was baptized in battle by an Indian attack.

When America entered the last war, MacArthur urged the development of a division composed of troops from every state in the union, to be called the Rainbow Division. A division was created, and Secretary of War Baker, recognizing unique organizing talents in the young leader, made him the Rainbow's chief of staff. When the war was over, Baker was to call him America's "greatest front-line fighting general."

Once in the field there was no holding him. He was twice wounded, once gassed. An attack on a machine gun nest in which he took part added an oak leaf cluster to the DSC he won, because, as the citation said "On a field where courage was the rule, his courage was the dominant feature." Disdaining helmet, gas mask, and sidearms, he once went with his men into No Man's Land, armed only with a riding crop. They brought back eight German prisoners, including a captain. MacArthur went along, he said, simply "to let the boys know somebody from headquarters was with them."

MacArthur's interest in sports won him the presidency of the American team that went to the Amsterdam Olympics in 1928. The manager of the American boxing team thought his men had got some raw decisions and threatened to withdraw from the remaining bouts. MacArthur ordered the team back to the ring with the words, "Americans don't quit."

In the fall of 1935, Philippine President Quezon approached MacArthur with the idea of going to the Islands as military adviser. MacArthur accepted. He stormed against those who thought the Islands indefensible.

When MacArthur took over, the Islands' defense forces consisted of 10,000 Philippine Scouts and Constabulary. His plan was to raise a conscript army of 40,000 a year, a ten years' total of 400,000. These men, trained at a military academy to be founded at Baguio, equipped with planes, and given sea protection with a fleet of motor torpedo boats, would do the trick, he thought.

MacArthur set out to instill in the Filipinos by word and action the highest military traditions. "Write your history in red on the breasts of your enemy" he told them. "Only those are fit to live who are not afraid to die for their country."

Before his plans could be completed, the Japs moved.

The blow at Pearl Harbor deprived MacArthur of protection he had every right to count on. In the face of ten to one superiority by an enemy who controlled sea and air, his courage and military genius have written one of the most inspiring pages in American history.

During the Manila attack an officer observed that the American flag on staff headquarters might serve as a target for Jap bombers and asked about removing it.

"Take every reasonable precaution," said MacArthur. "But let's keep the flag flying."

94

BATAAN: WHERE HEROES FELL
From *Time*[1]

"No Army has ever done so much with so little." In these words General Douglas MacArthur from Australia, where he had gone at the request of President Roosevelt, summed up the magnificent stand made by the United States–Philippine Army against overwhelming Japanese forces. The dogged courage with which the men on Bataan fought from their foxholes day after day until the end will be long remembered. This is the story of the last days and an interpretation of their meaning.

Bataan finally fell.

Bataan taught the U. S. a thing it had forgotten: pride of arms, pride in what the young men could do when tested.

Bataan taught America a humiliating thing, too: that U. S. soldiers could be beaten, could be taught the fullest shame of unconditional surrender. And they could be given this lesson by the funny pint-sized Jap—who, it suddenly appeared, was taut-muscled, courageous, vastly menacing.

The Jap had not changed. He was the same fellow who ran the curio shop in Rockefeller Center, or fished off California's coast. What had changed was a U. S. state of mind almost as old as the Republic. Before Pearl Harbor there was only one world to U. S. citizens. The world, the only world that Americans believed in or cared about, was the U. S. The rest of mankind was, in any

[1]From *Time*, April 20, 1942. Copyright, 1942, Time, Inc.

American sense, unreal. The American might—and did— throng the tourist spots like London and Paris, "Discover" Bali or the Dalmatian Coast, but he could never quite believe that these outlandish foreign parts could have a real connection with his world.

The Jap lived in the U. S. and worked against it, but his image was even mistier than the forms of the white men of Europe. Even after he had smashed at Pearl Harbor, his true form did not emerge. Americans did not yet believe what Pearl Harbor and Wake and Guam told them. They did not believe it because these first reverses of the war had a newsreel quality of unreality.

Bataan's end was different. Here was no blow that could be repaired in a navy yard. With Bataan went 36,000 or more courageous U. S. soldiers—heroes, three out of four of whom were sons of the Philippines. They had been worn to hollow shadows of men by fifteen days of smashing by the finest troops of the Son of Heaven. Because the U. S. had been well satisfied with the world it lived in, had pinched its boundless flood of pennies and sat alone, those U. S. soldiers had stumbled ragged, sleepless, and half-starved through the last days of the most humiliating defeat in U. S. history. In no previous battle had so many U. S. fighting men gone down before a foreign enemy, and seldom had any beaten U. S. soldiers been in such pitiable condition—believing until the last hour of destruction that their country could and surely would send them aid.

The U. S. had known the end was near. But it had not and could not, beforehand, taste the taste and smell the smell of crashing defeat.

The end was slow and agonizing and struck home the harder because Lieutenant General Jonathan M. Wainwright's communiqués were terse and professional. For fifteen days the Jap struck at Bataan with everything he had. Dive-bombers blew great craters in forward positions. Artillery roared endlessly day and night; the nervous chatter of Jap machine guns rattled until it rasped men's nerves like a file. The Jap even struck again at the hospital, scattered the wounded like straws.

Since the middle of January the men on Bataan had gone short of food. In Australia the Army had poured out good dollars to hire the adventurers of the South Seas to run the Jap blockade with food and ammunition. But nearly two out of three of the blockade-runners were lost —most of those, it seemed, which carried food.

Jonathan Wainwright's soldier's eye saw that the end was near. From the shores of the Bay he withdrew his naval forces, sailormen, and Marines of the 4th Regiment to Corregidor. He tried to strike one last blow. Against a Jap breakthrough on the Manila Bay side of the peninsula he threw a corps in desperate counter-attack. It was too much. The glassy-eyed soldiers went forward like men in a dream, so exhausted that many of them could hardly lift their feet, and the Jap mowed them down. The flank folded up.

The men on Corregidor saw only a little of the ghastly end. The last, pitifully small ammunition dump on Bataan went up in smoke and flame; the three ships at the water's edge were dynamited. Finally, from one of the heights on Bataan, a white flag went up. How many of the 36,000 died fighting, only the Japs knew.

Men still swam the shark-infested stretch from Bataan to Corregidor, and in the last few hours boats got across with nurses and a few survivors. But the biggest part of the battle-trained Philippine Army was gone. From the heights the Jap, with artillery already emplaced, began slamming away at Corregidor. The soldiers there and the few civilians who had fled from Bataan (where 20,000 had been an added charge on the troops) knew it could not be long before they were finished too. No gunners had ever been in finer positions than the Jap. From Bataan's heights he could pour fire night and day across two miles of water into Corregidor and see where every shell fell.

The survivors of the 9,000 American troops and 27,000 Filipinos fell into the hands of the Jap—all of them U. S. soldiers and U. S. losses. Alongside troops from the mainland, Tagalog and Moro and Igorot had fought just as bravely, died just as tight-lipped and with just as little fuss as their white comrades. It took that fighting and those deaths to make the U. S. know that the men from the Islands were their brothers and their equals.

In Australia Manuel Quezon [President of the Philippines] spoke the stout determination of the Islands, "The Filipino people will stand by America and our Allies to the bitter end. . . . I am profoundly grateful to the whole Army, which thus vindicated the honor and right of the Filipino people to become an independent nation."

They were all Americans on Bataan.

DOWN FLIGHT INTO JUNGLE

By an R.A.A.F. pilot[1]

One day an R.A.A.F. pilot took off from Australia on a reconnaissance flight over New Guinea. When, after nine days no word had been received from him at his headquarters, he was believed lost. The story of that nine days, however, he recorded in his diary.

Wednesday. About 3 P.M. At bottom of dive. Got big bump as though all bombs had gone off together. Took violent avoiding action and attempted to see results. Gunner rushed forward and said, "We're afire." Fire quickly got worse. Cabin filled with smoke, and flames obscured wing, so I yelled, "Go for your lives."

Beginning to get toasted. Attempted to open escape hatch. Unable to locate crew in smoke. Put on 'chute and tried to climb out window. Got stuck and stood on "stick." Aircraft dived steeply, so climbed in again and pulled nose up. Could not see for smoke, but at last managed to get through pilot's window and jumped sideways, shielding my head from the tailplane.

Tumbled over and over, but couldn't reach rip cord as 'chute was right out in front of me, and it was reversed. Eventually found rip cord and stopped with a bump. Trees rushed up at me. My "Mae West" was choking me and my head was forced back so I couldn't see the ground. Landed in trees. Realized I was choking, but was unable

[1]Used with the permission of The North American Newspaper Alliance.

to undo jacket. Nearly exhausted when I managed to struggle up to a higher bough and ease pressure.

Heard twigs breaking beneath me, and almost resigned to being taken by Japs. Turned out to be a wild pig. Lumps on my head, too, so I couldn't have missed the tailplane! Climbed gingerly down.

Lost lots of skin and landed in dense, dark jungle. Heard twigs breaking. Hid behind tree. Another pig.

Wednesday.—4 P.M. Walked on northwest course until I became thoroughly confused. Sat down and waited for stars, then set off through jungle again. Checking again found I had turned northeast. Sat down. Very thirsty. Only two matches in box and striker not much good. Mosquitoes nearly drove me mad, and wild pigs getting on my nerves. By licking leaves kept going until I found puddle. Drank cold water which made me feel sick. Found track leading west but struck mosquito-infested swamp. Climbed bank and lay down. Awake all night killing mosquitoes.

Thursday. Started again at dawn. Followed dry creeks toward coast, but time after time got cut off by impenetrable sword grass. Climbed back up steep mountains and cliffs. Only water cupped in leaves and pockets of fallen trees. Made about six attempts to reach sea but always blocked.

Sun got too high to judge direction so sat down and rested. Feeling weak from emptiness. Always thirsty. Made determined effort to follow small creek of stagnant water-holes to sea, irrespective of direction. Heard sea a long way off.

Reached sea at last. Took off clothes and lay in water. Perfect. Walked along beach. Came to wide river. Reached native village. They gave me bananas, paw paws, and water. Got feverish. Natives frightened to help me.

Set off again. Reached another village, tired and sick. Got three tabs of quinine and set off again. No water. Got hotter and hotter. Stagger on.

Find small puddle and drink. Full of pig marks but can hardly prevent myself lying down beside it and staying there. Reach beach and find Japs are in possession. Hurry back into jungle until I can go no further.

Friday. Reach white man's hut but no white man in it. Hundred yards on find white man in cave. So I meet Bill. Bill looked after me all day. Fed me coffee and marvelous soup. We meet Harold and discuss getting out. A Hudson comes over and drops flares. Try to signal with flash, which is hardly any good. We set out in Harold's Pinnace. Keep sharp lookout for Jap ships.

Monday. Meet another white man who gives us a sumptuous meal and a bath. Life seems grand again.

Tuesday. Walk a mile to visit another white man. He is alone. We talk to him about his schooner and spend some time camouflaging it.

Wednesday. It is now just a week since life seemed so desperate, swinging in my 'chute. We have worked all day loading the schooner. Near dusk we begin to move. The wind is blowing hard, and the crossing threatens to be hazardous.

Thursday. The crossing is hazardous. Seas break over us. There is a lot of water in the black hole of Calcutta we call the engine room. I am black with oil. The pumps won't work and we begin to bail. Water seems to be gaining. Weather seems to get worse.

Friday. Dawn, and there is no sight of land.

Friday. 1 P.M. Sight land. A pinnace rushed toward us. They might be Japs. But no, whacko, I can see Aussie hats.

*The eye at the periscope plays an important part in
submarine warfare*

A United States submarine on a practice run

SUBMARINE WARFARE IN THE
SOUTH PACIFIC

By a United States Submarine Commander. As told to George Weller[1]

Hunted continually by seaplanes, cruisers, and destroyers of the enemy, who knew that they were in the neighborhood, the submarine crew pressed home their attack, while their ears rang and the sub's hull shook with heavy depth charges. This story of a daring raid by a submarine of the United States Navy was told by its commander to Mr. Weller, as they sat upon a semitropical beach somewhere in the South Pacific.

"One night, having been upon the surface charging the batteries, my boat was preparing for a morning dive. We had been observed before by a Jap plane. Now we saw something on the port side.

"We were staring that way, when suddenly a brilliant beam of a searchlight jumped out of the darkness upon the starboard, illuminating us blindingly. While our attention was being drawn one way, another warship had crept in without being seen and spotted us. It was well planned, the second warship coming from the west, which direction was much darker than the dawning east.

"The searchlight did not have to sweep; it landed directly upon us. We dived for all we were worth. When we felt slightly less worried, we came up and took a peep.

[1]Somewhat condensed and edited. Used by special permission of The Chicago Daily News Foreign Service. Copyright, 1942, The Chicago Daily News, Inc.

"It was still too dark to see. The next peep we dared to take, we saw a destroyer tearing toward us. Down we went again. Soon propellers were overhead and depth charges began. We received a slight shaking up, but nothing comparable to what was coming."

As full daylight came, with the sun rising behind the clouds, the submarine captain gradually discerned a Jap naval force escorting not more than three transports. The fleet was almost of flattering proportions and included four destroyers, three cruisers, one with a big clipper bow and a painted white chrysanthemum as a figurehead.

The Jap preparations to handle the American submarine were careful and formidable. A big flagship patrolled watchfully in an east-west direction. The destroyers flashed here and there at a 15-knot pace, hunting actively.

Most significant of all, the three cruiser seaplane catapults were empty, and two seaplanes could be seen patrolling both the harbor and the waters around.

"I went in anyway, upon the big cruiser," said the commander. "The transports were already inside the harbor unloading. The breeze gave me good periscope protection, and I let go from the forward tubes. Between two torpedo releases I saw the Japs running wildly about upon the quarterdeck. Then I plunged. More than a minute ticked off upon my watch, then came a very heavy explosion.

"It took the Japs less than three minutes to begin depth-charging us. It sounded as though hundreds of depth-charges were going off. They came much faster than they could be counted. How near were they? Well, the depth gauge whipped far around, the engine blowers danced, and we got a couple of leaks."

Hour after hour, the submarine traveled slowly forward upon her batteries. Sometimes the charges were so heavy that they almost caused the notebook of the quartermaster, who was keeping count, to leap from his hand.

The attack had occurred early in the morning. It was mid-afternoon before the constant sounds of hunting began to grow fainter and the propellers overhead became more inaudible.

After going deep, to gain distance and safety, the sub arose again for another peek. A cruiser and a destroyer, still hunting her, were less than three miles away.

The moon was approaching full and all the crew, despite the battering, wished to return to the attack. The destroyer and the cruiser were tempting targets. But the slender hull already reeked of dangerous explosive hydrogen from overuse of the batteries during the day. It was time for caution rather than daring.

The almost irresistible quarry was rejected, and the patient labor of recharging continued. There must have been a Santa Claus riding the skies that night. Another Jap cruiser appeared, circling cautiously, about five miles away.

The submarine had big plans, but only a few torpedoes left. After making devious calculations which are necessary to bring a creeping submarine across the course of a galloping cruiser, the sub furtively cut off the big Jap and turned her rear upon him. The stern tubes belched torpedoes.

"I heard one very violent explosion in less than a minute," said the commander. "The other officers claim two, and it's sometimes hard to tell another torpedo exploding from internal explosion. But I'll string along with one.

"Anyway, I could see his propellers stopped. He was coasting. His speed kept falling. We saw he was pouring smoke from the stacks, seeming to indicate that things were going wrong down below.

"The next look we took, he had disappeared. We never heard his propellers again."

But submarine crews attacking warships never get the same chance to sit back and congratulate themselves, afterward, that submarines, hitting merchant ships without depth charges, enjoy. The stricken cruiser must have sent a call for help, for "Sound," suddenly a lookout shouted up, "High speed ship approaching from southwest," and almost immediately the enemy was overhead. But apparently deciding not to slam the barndoor too hard after the horse had been stolen, the warships overhead made a relatively moderate depth-charge attack.

Should the submarine now make her escape? Not while any tubes in her hull still remained full of "fish."

"Again we closed for harbor," said the commander, kicking the sand around our feet. "Soon we saw ship tops and right afterward they developed into four destroyers, two cruisers, and one seaplane.

"A cruiser's plane catapult was already empty, indicating that they were looking for us. It was a little after daybreak. The other cruiser plane took off and began hunting for us. The whole gang of them were looking

106

for us under water, on the surface, and overhead. We kept watching for our chance.

"About four o'clock in the afternoon, a cruiser entered the harbor and circled around the transports, flying signal flags and transmitting visual orders. Then a pair of destroyers began patrolling an East-West line of the harbor's mouth while the other two took up escort positions upon the other side of the cruiser.

"Sweeping our periscope around, we found ourselves in the center of a rectangle of warships. Every last one of them was trying to find us.

"It was like being in the middle of a shooting gallery.

"Then the big cruiser decided to leave for healthier waters. Any warship's zig-zags are unpredictable, yet the whole success of a submarine's attack depends upon their breaking right.

"The first gave me a moderate angle. Then he took the angle away. It looked as though I'd lose him. I said a prayer. At precisely the right moment, he turned and started a new zig-zag leg.

"By this time I figured it was probably the same cruiser I had aimed at before, and that the explosion must have been a fish hitting one of the transports at anchor in the cove beyond. When he gave me that third angle, it was the answer to my prayer.

"I gave him everything that was left in the tubes. The distance was less than a mile. At precisely the right moment, when expected, came a terrific explosion. Then everybody went for us. In a minute by my watch, after the explosion, the Japs were dumping all the ashcans upon their decks onto our heads. You never heard such a chorus of propellers and depth-charges; it was a regular orchestral suite.

"They sat for hours above us, throwing depth bombs in every direction. But God was working for us. At a dangerous depth, there came a friendly current sweeping us off without the tell-tale use of our motors. Due to our sudden dive, our hydrogen content was again dangerously high. Everybody was barefoot, carrying buckets and bailing several inches of water from the bottom of the hull and pouring it into waste tanks. This hand method of pumping worked. There were still ships all around, but finally they grew fainter, and late into the night, and far away from the doomed harbor, we arose and felt the wind blow in our faces. Our tubes were empty; our job was done; and we were headed for home."

I HAVE A SCORE TO SETTLE

By *Stanley Hope*, Pilot Officer, R.A.F. By air mail
from London[1]

They came in on him from all directions. The plane was
hit. The pilot was injured. The nose of the plane was heading
toward the sea. This unusual story of an aerial combat was
written by the pilot in the hospital at the request of the medical
officer attending him. The medical officer was anxious to know
as accurately as possible all the details of the combat, particu-
larly the pilot's thoughts and sensations during it.

We were on one of the usual offensive sweeps—a daylight
raid on some works near Lille, and during a widespread
dog fight over the target I chased a 109 down several
thousand feet but lost him in a cloud. Pulling up to regain
my height I found the sky completely empty.

I hung around for a few minutes feeling like the only
living thing in space and then started home alone at
18,000 feet, weaving hard and losing height gradually to
keep my speed up.

I had a clear run as far as St. Omer, where two 109F's
passed 1000 feet above me and slightly to the left, going
the opposite way. I was then at 13,000 feet.

I climbed into the sun, intending to beat up these two
as soon as I could be quite sure they were alone. Instantly
the trap sprung; 109's came down on me from every
corner of the sky and in no time I was the center of a

[1]Used with the permission of The North American Newspaper
Alliance.

large gaggle, consisting of nine or ten Messerschmitts and one Spitfire—mine!

I didn't care for the look of things and felt a bit anxious, although not actually frightened. I was acutely keyed up and highly interested. I hardly ever remember feeling frightened once a fight has started, though frequently on other occasions.

I took terrific evasive action and the Huns did a lot of inaccurate shooting. The job was hectic, but as the fight went on and on, I became greatly encouraged by their failure, so far, to hit me.

I fired a short burst at half deflection at a 109E and knocked pieces from his radiator, releasing a stream of glycol. Then I saw it was nothing more than glycol. I hoped the thing would catch fire or explode. I was very angry; I am always angry with the Luftwaffe and passionately desire its total extermination. However, the 109 went spiralling down out of sight, still streaming glycol. I think it was under control and probably it was successfully forced landed.

I then tried to outclimb all the 109's into the sun in order to start attacking from out of it. I have many times seen large German formations routed by very few English machines, so it seemed worth trying, and there might be one or two stooges who would give me a target.

It didn't work. Four 109's which had stayed above me all the time saw what I was up to, climbed in the same direction, and remained above. There were too many of them!

As my gas was limited and we were still well inside France I decided to concentrate on getting home intact, and with continuous and violent evasive action, I moved westward to the French coast hoping to meet some friendly fighters which I knew were somewhere in that direction. I was beginning to tire a little and was certainly getting fed up with this tomfoolery, which had now gone on for about twenty minutes, and I would greatly have welcomed some help or at any rate a few seconds breathing space. I felt terribly lonely.

As we neared the coast just north of Hardelot the tactical disposition of the 109's, which, of course, was changing every second, suddenly took on a dangerous aspect, and in turning to fox an attack by two of them which were coming in from the port side, I gave a momentary opening for two more to close in behind me. Before I could rectify this a series of loud metallic bangs occurred, and large holes, appearing first in the starboard wing tip, swept straight inboard to the fuselage. Although I could watch each hole appearing individually it all happened in a split second. Then there was a deafening bang inside the cockpit and something feeling like a steam hammer hit me on the back of the head and knocked me out.

I don't think I entirely lost consciousness, or if I did, it was only for a very few seconds; but total darkness descended and every ounce of energy left me. I hadn't enough to move my little finger. I felt myself fading away as though under an anaesthetic. I was conscious of nothing but utter darkness and a pain behind my right ear. But a tiny corner of my mind, outside everything else, was still functioning, and I remember soliloquizing, detachedly, in the dark,—"So after all it's happened to me too. . . . It's come to you, who have always told yourself there's some way out of every scrape. But there's no way out of this one, Buddy, because you are quite blind and you haven't the strength to move a muscle and you are diving down helplessly towards the sea at an enormous speed with a lot of 109's on your tail ready to polish you off very quickly if you show any signs of revival. So there! . . . I wish I could have had a word with the chaps, just to explain how it happened, instead of simply vanishing like so many others. . . . And there are such a lot of people I'd like to have said goodbye to. . . . And you're a clown to be shot down by a ——— Hun anyway. . . . But it's too late for regrets now. . . . It can only be a few seconds now. . . . Just one almighty holocaust as we hit the sea. . . . Then. . . . No more of this nightmare flight, no more pain at the back of the head; just peace. . . . How marvelous! And I haven't got a date tonight anyway, so there isn't that to fuss about."

I knew the speed was very high. You can tell by a sort of hard feeling and the sound of the wind. I was completely resigned now, and hardly at all frightened. Regretful, yes. But I wasn't frightened, for I knew I was so nearly unconscious that I wouldn't feel much of the impact when the airplane hit the sea.

A few seconds more darkness ticked serenely by. As there was nothing I could do I need make no effort. It was wonderful to have to make no effort. Except for the pain in my head the relaxation was sheer bliss.

Then consciousness began creeping back. With a major effort I pulled the radio lever to "transmit," called out my squadron number, and said "Cheerio, Binto, I'm just going into the sea." (Binto was the ground station.)

Then I began to notice something. My world of darkness was no longer black; it was turning red. Very dimly, as through ultra dark red glasses I began to make out the nose of the Spitfire, pointing straight down towards a hazy, dark red sea.

I thought, "I'm coming round! Now I've got to try and fly again."

Two seconds later I was fully conscious and mentally screaming at myself, "Wake up, you silly clot! Wake up! You're not dead yet and the machine may still fly for all you know. You may get out of even this scrape if you wake up and pull yourself together!"

With a physical reluctance which I have previously known only at the height of a critical illness, I began to pull the Spitfire out of the dive, weaving all the time. She was mushy and sluggish, so I knew that the elevators had been hit. The 109's came down on me like a ton of bricks, shooting so prolifically that it was almost funny. The sky was full of the vicious little smoke spirals from their guns and the streak of tracer shells. I did everything I could to upset their aim, and their shooting was wild.

I held an erratic dive down to 1,000 feet for the sake of speed. I had to keep forcing myself to go on flying, though the actual control of the aircraft was instinctive as long as my hands and feet would consent to function at all.

There was blood all over the place. I am not affected by the sight of blood, or not my own anyway, but I knew I was losing rather a lot.

The Spitfire was slow because of its injuries, which was galling, as a Mark V is normally faster than a 109 at sea level. Two or three times when the Huns got too close, I had to turn and mix it with them for a little while to stop them closing right in on my tail, but gradually—very gradually it seemed—we approached England.

By now the redness had faded out and colors were normal again.

Some of the 109's turned back, perhaps out of ammunition, and only five continued chasing me. My head was swimming, and I had to keep fighting a tremendous longing to flop forward and plunge straight into the sea.

I was heading for the nearest forward airdrome, just inside the coast, and I hoped to lead the 109's over it and let the ground defences have a crack at them, but six or eight miles from the English coast they all turned back.

My mind went round and round and started arguing three ways at once. One part of it said, "Here's your chance; you've got them cold now; get after them for all you're worth. One or two may be lagging, and it'd be grand to get one now." Another part quickly swamped this with a most ardent revulsion from any sort of effort whatsoever. A third part, functioning sanely, said, "Don't be even stupider than you are. You've lost a fair amount of blood and if you hang around now you may pass out. Besides the plane is too slow anyway. Down you get on to the ground immediately."

As I saw the 109's disappearing I remember thinking, "Well, how many of you does it take to shoot a Spitfire down?" which was very foolish, considering it sometimes takes only one.

So I made for the coastal airdrome. On arrival there I thought the effort of flying to the downwind end would be more than I could manage. I felt hideously sick and too exhausted even to think. I could feel myself growing weaker every second, and I wondered whether I could land before fainting. Blood was streaming down my neck and the control column was covered with it and all sticky. I longed to flop forward and dive straight into the deck— and oblivion.

I had to screw up all my determination to lower the wheels, and once again to lower the flaps, though each operation requires only the movement of a light lever.

As I held off to land I brightened up a little, knowing the job was nearly done, and with infinite concentration made quite a decent landing.

I taxied in and stopped. With a final effort, which was nothing but a concession to my own pride, I checked over the cockpit with great thoroughness to see that I'd left all the switches, etc. as they should be left. Gingerly I eased off my helmet, and grinned to a friend from my own squadron who had dropped in for some fuel. He grinned back and then realizing that things weren't too good he shouted boisterously for the ambulance.

I remember his stirring comments when someone produced a fire engine instead. But the ambulance was quite quick.

When I woke up ten hours later in hospital it was with the happy realization that there was nothing more to do but get better again.

I felt frightful, admittedly. But I was in England among friends, and not, as I might easily have been, in German hands in France. Nothing else mattered, and the relief that I felt was past description.

They had operated on my head and dug out numerous little bits of metal casing from the cannon shell which had exploded far too close for my liking.

I've got the bits at home and I am keeping them. One day they will help me shoot a good line to my grand-children. But before then there is a score to settle. That Hun certainly gave me a very sore head, and I want above all a chance to hand it back. I'll be a lot happier after that.

SHOVELS TO HAND GRENADES

From *The Boston Globe*[1]

"Get in the scrap." It's your country calling, and the call is answered by millions of people all over the land—school children, farmers, manufacturers, housewives, office workers. Today they are old fences, rails, bridges, springs, wheels, beds, metal toys, auto parts, kitchen sinks, lawn mowers, sheets, towels, ropes, tires, tennis shoes. Tomorrow they will be ships and tanks and planes and guns, fighting for democracy all over the world. Let's visit a big junk yard and see what happens to metal scrap there.

The first thing you see, as you draw near, is huge piles of scrap metal; there are acres of these piles—nine to be exact —at the yard we're visiting. The twisted metal and broken heaps of machinery look like a mechanic's nightmare.

Then, dominating the center of the yard, you see the immense 110-foot derrick. It's lifting whole truck loads of broken metal, shifting it to the machines that prepare the scrap for shipment to the foundries. The derrick can pick up fifty tons of the stuff in a straight lift.

There are two coughing, steam-belching locomotive cranes at work; one with a magnetic lift. They'll handle ten to fifteen tons at one time and can be moved all over the yard.

Next you notice the overalled workers. In normal times there are 125 of them at this particular yard; but,

[1]From *The Boston Evening Globe*, October 6, 1942. Copyright, 1942, Globe Newspaper Co.

these days, due to the scarcity of help, there are only 80—trying to do the work of 160. They all try to put in at least fifty hours in a week.

The first workers you see are four men who are operating the biggest pair of alligator shears in the yard. These shears stick out of the power house that drives them, looking much like an alligator's head, and the illusion is made more striking by the automatic manner in which they open and close their great jaws.

As the jaws munch up and down, the four workmen feed them prodigious amounts of steel and iron. It's dangerous work—that top blade weighs two tons and it'll bite through a solid steel axle that's more than three inches through. Imagine what it would do to the careless hand or arm that got in its way!

You go next to the bigger of the two hydraulic presses at the yard. You look down into a pit that's about as big as the grease pit at an automobile service station. The workers call it the baling press, and your eyes pop out as you watch them toss whole automobile bodies into the pit and fill in the chinks with iron barrels and other pieces of sheet metal, and then see the press compress all that metal into cubes that are $14 \times 14 \times 18$ inches and weigh about 600 pounds apiece.

The press has a three-way squeeze, each pressing wall of which has 300 tons of pressure behind it. A skilled operator sits in a little control room in front and above the press and works the levers that bring the great pressure to bear. You learn that he can turn out 225 of those 600-pound cubes a day.

The yard foreman tells you that the yard can handle

118

Three patriotic junior-high-school scrap collectors

Aft gun mount aboard a Coast Guard cutter[1]

[1]Reprinted by special permission of the *Saturday Evening Post*; copyright by the Curtis Publishing Company, 1942.

about 200 tons of scrap a day. The metal cubes are piled in freight cars as fast as they are compressed. The solid pieces going through the shears are piled in other cars. No piece of the solid stuff can go to the foundry if it's more than eighteen inches in length.

A shower of sparks calls your attention to one of the acetylene-torch wielders. He's working on a huge tank that wouldn't fit into any cutting machine; his blasting flame breaks it up into the right size pieces.

You take a peek at the lead furnaces before you leave. One is of the reverbatory type, and it'll melt ten tons a day; the second is a blast furnace that will handle twenty-five tons.

The lead is obtained from old automobile batteries. It pours from the furnaces into a huge twenty-ton kettle and then is ladled out into 75-pound ingots. Workmen are piling a rush Navy load in a freight car, while we watch.

Your faith in American ingenuity is restored when you learn the reason for a huge pile of clamshells near the furnaces. You are told that lime for the furnaces could not be obtained, and the important Navy work was in danger of being stalled. But the foreman investigated, found out that clamshells were largely composed of lime, and made arrangements for huge quantities of them to feed his furnaces.

And the work goes on!

I TEST TANK TRAPS

By *Sergeant James M. Hayden*, Tank Co., 29th
Division. As told to Frederick C. Painton[1]

At Fort Belvoir, Virginia, men and machines engage in a
gigantic obstacle race, unique in that both the tank-drivers and
the obstacles are trying to win. Engineers of the United States
Army gouge great holes out of the earth with dynamite, throw
up bridges, plant fields with steel rails, mass barricades of logs.
They are given exactly one hour and a half to build a road
obstacle or trap, and their purpose is to build it strong enough
to stop a tank cold. Runners in this race are the tank-drivers.
Their purpose is to take their iron monsters over the obstacle.
Tough? It looked deadly, was Sergeant Hayden's thought
when he took his first look at a tank obstacle which he was to
test. Logs twenty inches thick and longer than telephone poles
had been piled five feet high and tied together with half-inch
steel cable. Three huge logs, like a three-pronged spear, pro-
jected from them—and directly at him. Could he get over it?
Well, he could try. After all he was well aware that no trap-
tester has ever refused to hit any obstacle.

A whistle shrilled. The engineer lieutenant ordered his
men off the block, told them, no matter what happened to
the tank, they were to stand quiet.

"O. K., sergeant," called Captain Daman. "Button her
up and slam it."

I slid into the seat. Technician Ralph Elliott fastened

[1]From *Liberty*, June 27, 1942. Used with the permission of
Liberty. Copyright, 1942, Macfadden Publications, Inc.

the turret tops, closed the front plates. Blackness now, except for the narrow vision slit through the armor.

I saw Raleigh Boaze go down near the hurdles, carrying a fire extinguisher. There was one near my hand, but in case the tank turned over, caught fire, and I got knocked cold, they could control the flames and get me out unbroiled.

Last-minute check. Safety belt tight. Old-style helmet firm to protect my skull. Then Corporal Bob Weaver waved his hand. O.K! This was it.

I gave the foot siren a punch, and it screamed a warning. I threw the clutch, got into second gear, and the tank began to blitz. Immediately I was no longer nervous. I felt fine. Nothing could stop this baby!

Swiftly I got her into fourth gear with maybe twenty-five yards to go to the nearest hurdle. I got a tight grip on the two control levers. The speedometer needle hit twenty-five! Thirty! The obstacle, big as a mountain now, blocked out all else.

WHAM!

A heavy weight thrust on my shoulder. The world vanished. All I could see through my slit was blue sky and lovely clouds. The tank had hit the hurdle, was nose up in the air. Crash! The second hurdle. A reeling world. Was she going to turn over? I braced instinctively, jammed the accelerator pedal to the floor. I remember saying, "Come on, baby, don't let me down." But I couldn't have heard my own voice. The roar of the 250 horses of radial motor inside that tank would have drowned out anything.

Now, for a split second, the tank was level. The deadly

spear points of logs rushed at me. A rumbling crash. One log end had caught the door plate on the right side, had torn it off, and started to come through the hole. Then it vanished. The inside was full of light. The tank was pawing up the air. She lurched over on her side, one tread grabbed at thin air. She flopped back with a smash as a log gave way. The safety belt sawed at my waist. The tank was pushing a log with her turret, and it blocked my vision. I could see nothing and guided her by the seat of my pants. Now a tread was spinning on air. I pulled the right control lever to give more power to the contact tread.

Another log gave way behind. I seemed to be on my back. Was she going to turn over backward? The rubber pad on the slope plate jumped at my chin. The tank had stopped with a smash. Level but not moving. I poured on the coal. But both treads apparently were clawing the air. I was stopped!

The engineer platoon was cheering and yelling and laughing. A few of them were pretending to aim a .37-millimeter antitank gun to blow me and the tank to bits. Now I could see that the tank's belly rested on a huge log that held her high so the treads had no traction.

Captain Daman was grinning. "Tough luck, sergeant! If you could have dodged that center log you could have gone through." And he went off to explain to the engineer lieutenant the good and bad qualities of the obstacle.

Tank obstacles and tank traps are used both defensively and offensively. Suppose an attacking army commander, taking his troops along a main highway, wanted to be sure that the enemy could not use parallel roads on either

122

side to drive in with a tank force and flank him. He would assign engineers to put in road blocks and tank traps that must stop them. The engineers would seek out a defile—a place on the road where steep embankments or slopes prevent the tanks from going around. Here tank traps can be made by blowing deep craters in the road, or, if there is nearby woodland, various types of log obstacles can be built.

Suppose the commanding officer should decide to blow a crater. How could he be certain it would trap and stop a tank?

Witness such a test. The crater was seventeen feet in depth and twenty-one feet across. The defense side was so steep that once the tank plunged into the crater, it could not paw down enough earth to pull out. Also, if the tank couldn't leap the gap, it would go, nose down, into solid earth. And the terrific shock of an instantaneous stop from thirty miles an hour would probably injure or kill the driver and disable the tank. It was up to me and my light tank to see what would happen.

The ground was dry and there was a slight down grade. As against this, however, the side of the crater toward the enemy was not built up but sloped in, so the tank could not get a jumping take-off. This was a problem of speed and momentum.

I was making thirty-six miles an hour when the tank reached the lip of the crater. Those who watched said later that the tank seemed to hang in the air, not rising. I had the sensation she wouldn't make it. I felt myself trying mentally to lift her. There was a terrific rocking crash—but two feet or so of her treads reached the mound

123

on the other side. I had the accelerator to the floor. She stood on her tail, but the treads grabbed and shot her over to safety.

This proved one fact: a road crater twenty-one feet wide will not stop a tank unless you put hurdles or obstacles in front of it to prevent the tank getting full momentum for the jump.

When tank-trap testing was first begun at Fort Belvoir, the traps and obstacles were so easy that we were rarely stopped. Learning the realistic way, the engineers soon made them very tough indeed. One day we hit eight—with daring drivers—and our tanks were stopped cold.

To understand just what "stopped cold" means, take the experience of my predecessor, Sergeant Bill Cochran of the Lightning First of Fort Knox, Kentucky.

The rookie platoons had worked like beavers on the job Bill was to test. They had not only built three tough hurdles and an asparagus bed (planted heavy steel rails) but had also constructed a V-type crib obstacle which consists of an arrowshaped pile of logs with the point aimed at you. Behind that was a sawhorse or ramp type, where the tank is supposed to get hung up on its belly with no traction for treads.

It was a dry day; the runway was fine, downhill slightly, and about a third of a mile long. When Bill set his siren screaming and took off, he had top speed in a few yards. He was making a full thirty-six miles an hour when he struck the first hurdle—going so fast, indeed, that the medium tank leaped ten feet in the air as it hit the first hurdle.

It stayed in the air for thirty-one feet (we measured it

124

later) and entirely jumped the asparagus bed. It skimmed the crib and came down on the sawhorse.

There was a terrific crash like a clap of thunder. The ground actually trembled. One instant that twenty-one tons of steel was racing at thirty miles an hour. The next, it was stopped still. We raced up and got the turret unbuttoned.

Bill said, "That hurdle shock knocked the ignition switch off. I didn't have any power. Let me take another whack at her."

Men new to war must learn the hard way. Just recently a pontoon bridge was built, supposed to be able to carry the weight of light tanks. I took one look and saw it wasn't built properly. But the makers had to be shown. I drove the tank onto the bridge. It promptly collapsed and dumped me neck-high into some five feet of water. The cooling fan of the engine acted as a self-bailer for the engine housing, and I poured on the coal and drove out of there. The new pontoon bridge *will* hold light and medium tanks if correctly built.

Sure we're guinea pigs. Our driving gets tested and so do our tanks. We have become better drivers for the experience. The casualties are far between. And, of course, we've all passed the tough tank driver's test—you know, the one where they test you for quick reflexes, balance, resistance to dizziness, width of vision (on account of the narrow vision slit when a tank is buttoned up), and ability to gauge swiftly the relation of two objects to each other.

When a tank takes off and you go out of this world into the blue sky, you've got to handle your balance by instinct, maneuver by feel, and learn to know what a tank will do by looking at the terrain.

On a recent jump in which his tank was in the air only a split second, Technician Ralph Elliott changed from fourth to third gear, and never knew he had done it.

Finally, you get to know tanks and what they'll take. You have a fierce pride in them. They're tough, they'll take anything, go anywhere. And you get a lot of pride in yourself. We have never refused to hit any trap. We never will.

Man, O man, when Captain Daman says, "Sock her," and I punch the siren and pour on the oil, no bunch of engineers who ever lived could stop me and **my** tank.

BRAVE MEN AND A FIGHTING SHIP

Excerpts from radio talks by *Franklin D. Roosevelt*[1]

"I wish that all the American people could read all the citations for various medals recommended for our soldiers, sailors, and Marines."—Franklin D. Roosevelt. Here are stories of four men and a once lost ship, as President Roosevelt told them.

There is, for instance, Dr. Corydon M. Wassell. He was a missionary, well-known for his good works in China. He is a simple, modest, retiring man, nearly sixty years old, but he entered the services of his country and was commissioned a lieutenant-commander in the navy.

Dr. Wassell was assigned to duty in Java, caring for wounded officers and men of the cruisers *Houston* and *Marblehead* which had been in heavy action in the Java seas.

When the Japanese advanced across the island it was decided to evacuate as many as possible of the wounded to Australia. But about twelve of the men were so badly wounded that they could not be moved. Dr. Wassell remained with these men, knowing that he would be captured by the enemy.

But he decided to make a desperate attempt to get the men out of Java. He asked each of them if he wished to take the chance and everyone agreed.

He first had to get the twelve men to the seacoast fifty miles away. To do this he had to improvise stretchers

[1]From radio talks by Franklin Delano Roosevelt, President of the United States, April 28, September 7, and October 12, 1942.

for the hazardous journey. The men were suffering severely, but Dr. Wassell kept them alive by his skill and inspired them by his own courage.

As the official report said, Dr. Wassell was "almost like a Christ-like shepherd devoted to his flock."

On the seacoast he embarked the men on a little Dutch ship. They were bombed and machine-gunned by waves of Japanese planes. Dr. Wassell took virtual command of the ship and by great skill avoided destruction, hiding in small bays and inlets.

A few days later Dr. Wassell and his little flock of wounded men reached Australia safely.

Dr. Wassell now wears the navy cross.

You may remember the tragic sinking of the submarine *Squalus* off the New England coast in the summer of 1939. Some of the men were lost, but others were saved by the speed and efficiency of the surface rescue crews. The *Squalus* itself was tediously raised from the bottom of the ocean.

Eventually she sailed again under a new name, the U.S.S. *Sailfish*. Today she is a potent and effective unit of our submarine fleet.

She has sunk a Japanese destroyer.

She has torpedoed a Japanese cruiser.

She has made two torpedo hits on a Japanese aircraft carrier.

Three of the enlisted men of our navy who went down with the *Squalus* in 1939 are today serving on the same ship, the *Sailfish*, in this war.

It is heartening to know that the *Squalus*, once given up as lost, was raised from the depths to fight for our country in time of peril.

This is the story of one of our army Flying Fortresses, operating in the western Pacific. The pilot of this plane is a modest young man, proud of his crew for one of the toughest fights a bomber has yet experienced.

The bomber departed from its base, as part of a flight of five, to attack Japanese transports that were landing troops in the Philippines.

When they had gone about halfway to their destination, one of the motors of his bomber went out of commission. The young pilot lost contact with the other bombers. The crew, however, got the motor working again, and the plane proceeded on its mission alone.

By the time it arrived at its target, the other four Flying Fortresses had already passed over, had dropped their bombs, and had stirred up the Japanese Zero planes.

Eighteen attacked our one Flying Fortress. Despite this mass attack, our plane proceeded on its mission and dropped all of its bombs on six Japanese transports which were lined up along the docks.

As it turned back on its homeward journey a running fight between the bomber and the 18 Japanese pursuit planes continued for 75 miles. Four pursuit ships attacked simultaneously at each side and were shot down with side guns. During this fight the bomber's radio operator was killed, the engineer's right hand was shot off, and one gunner was crippled, leaving only one man available to operate both side guns. Although wounded in one hand, this gunner alternately manned both side guns, bringing down three more Japanese Zero planes.

While this was going on, one engine of the bomber was shot out, one gas tank was hit, the radio was shot off, and the oxygen system was entirely destroyed. Out of eleven control cables all but four were shot away. The rear landing wheel was blown off, and the two front wheels were shot flat.

With two engines gone and the plane practically out of control, the American bomber returned to its base after dark and made an emergency landing.

The mission had been accomplished.

The name of that pilot is Captain Hewitt T. Wheless, of the United States Army. He comes from Menard, Texas—population 2,375. He has been awarded the Distinguished Service Cross. I hope he is listening.[1]

I wish that all the American people could read all the citations for various medals recommended for our soldiers, sailors, and Marines. I am picking out one of these citations which tells of the accomplishments of Lieutenant John James Powers, United States Navy, during three days of the battles with Japanese forces in the Coral Sea.

During the first two days, Lieutenant Powers, flying a dive-bomber in the face of blasting enemy anti-aircraft fire, demolished one large enemy gunboat, put another gunboat out of commission, severely damaged an aircraft tender and a 20,000-ton transport, and scored a direct hit on an aircraft carrier which burst into flames and sank soon after.

The official citation describes the morning of the third day of battle. As the pilots of his squadron left the ready room to man their planes, Lieutenant Powers said to them,

[1]He was. With his wife and daughter in Fresno, California, he listened to the President's speech.

"Remember, the folks back home are counting on us. I am going to get a hit if I have to lay it on their flight deck."

He led his section down to the target from an altitude of 18,000 feet, through a wall of bursting anti-aircraft shells and swarms of enemy planes. He dived almost to the very deck of the enemy carrier, and did not release his bomb until he was sure of a direct hit. He was last seen attempting recovery from his dive at the extremely low altitude of 200 feet, amid a terrific barrage of shell and bomb fragments, smoke, flame, and debris from the stricken vessel. His own plane was destroyed by the explosion of his own bomb. But he had made good his promise to "lay it on the flight deck."

I have received a recommendation from the Secretary of the Navy that Lieutenant James Powers, of New York city, missing in action, be awarded the Medal of Honor. I hereby and now make this award.

In expanding our shipping, we have had to enlist many thousands of men for our merchant marine. These men are serving magnificently. They are risking their lives every hour so that guns and tanks and planes and ammunition and food may be carried to the heroic defenders of Stalingrad and to all the United Nations' forces all over the world.

A few days ago I awarded the first maritime distinguished service medal to a young man—Edward F. Cheney of Yeadon, Pennsylvania—who had shown great gallantry in rescuing his comrades from the oily waters of the sea after their ship had been torpedoed. There will be many more such acts of bravery.

ABOARD A COAST GUARD CUTTER

By *Charles Rawlings*[1]

She was built as a 165-foot United States Coast Guard Cutter in 1934. Now she is a submarine-chaser with a crew of fifty-five, with depth-charge racks over the stern, a depth charge Y-gun on the quarter deck, a 3-inch 25 bow rifle, and two 20-mm. quick-firing machine guns throwing shrapnel. Her beat is one of the toughest—the western Atlantic. Within six months of war she had the record in her district for blowing the most holes in the ocean with the most depth charges per ship per hour at sea. This is chiefly the story of *Diana* the Huntress, as Mr. Rawlings calls her, and Frisky.

It had been a sunny afternoon late in the winter. Everything except the German was pretty harum-scarum up and down the coast. Jerry with most of his U-boat fleet was having his fun while he could. *Diana*, along with the rest of the overworked, thin line of ready vessels on patrol off the capes, was ordered to help coastwise shipping around Torpedo Junction, Cape Hatteras, whenever she could be spared. She had a little flock of boats this sunny afternoon, and being alone, she decided to put them in double column and run long diagonals across their front. All had gone well around Hatteras, and they had come on Wimble Shoals.

In *Diana's* engine room at that time was Frisky, fireman, third class. Frisky is a curly-headed, average, wise-

[1]From *We Saw the Battle of the Atlantic.* Copyright, 1942, by Charles Rawlings. Copyright, 1942, The Curtis Publishing Company.

cracking American kid of twenty-three or twenty-four. He sings a good lead baritone, and all hands like him. He was having a bit of trouble getting adjusted to the engine room, however. The below-decks stations on a submarine chaser require a particular type of nerves. You're shut in and cannot see what is happening, except when it happens, and then you see it all at once, with the whole side coming in, nicely lighted up by the blinding flash of a torpedo.

Every moment he was free, and sometimes when he wasn't, Frisky was up the engine-room ladder straining out over the sea. That sunny afternoon on Wimble Shoals, Frisky, up the ladder, saw a spurt of white water. There were whitecaps up to weather, and what Frisky saw might have been one, for an ordinary lookout. Not for Frisky. He locked the spot in his squinting eyes and strained on. There was another upflung, quick splatter. A porpoise might have made such a splash. Frisky doesn't trust porpoises. There were three quick spurts of white in succession. "Lippity, lippity, lippity." Frisky had seen spurts like those in his dreams. He knew what they were.

"Torpedo!" he screamed. "Look!" He was out the hatch and down the deck now, bumping into things and scrambling up and scurrying on toward the bridge. "A torpedo! See it! See it!"

The captain, the watch officer, the flying-bridge look-outs and the quartermaster followed his wild eyes. Torpedo it was. It was shallow set, speeding at forty knots, and angled beautifully for *Diana*.

Diana swung up into the projectile's course, and laid on her whistle to warn the lead ship in the convoy, a rusty tanker, that she was lumbering up into danger.

The tanker understood and reversed her engines. *Diana* and the ugly thing passed twenty yards apart, going in opposite directions. The too-slow tanker, just gathering way astern, caught it smack on the water line directly under the port wing of the bridge. It blew a column of black oil and deck plates and bridge high into the air. *Diana* carried on at full throttle to meet Wimble Willy.

The sound gear had its sharp ear pressed tightly against him. Wimble Willy had gone to ground and was frantically trying to hide there. His bold plan—to destroy *Diana* and then take his time with the slow tankers—had changed, because of Frisky, to a fight to save his own skin. He very likely was hearing *Diana's* big propellers by this time through his hydrophones. If so, he heard her gaining, heard her circling, heard her square off for her run, heard the propellers overhead, and then the explosion of the Y-gun propelling charge shooting its cans off *Diana's* quarters. Other cans roll off the stern racks. The barrage enclosed him like a noose of earthquakes, and he stopped, in all probability, hearing all things.

The first attack brought up oil. It is no longer considered proof of a kill. It may mean only that the enemy has thrown off a charge of it, or it may mean that one, or both, of a pair of saddle fuel tanks carried outside the main submarine hull has collapsed. *Diana* made run after run, changing the pattern of the depth charges.

At last, with her racks nearly empty—a ship must not disarm herself completely—*Diana* rigged a buoy and sent its anchor down, and turned him over to the planes and the Navy. She found her crippled tanker back on the course, limping on at three knots.

And Frisky—

"He came to me," said the captain, "and said very humbly that, in his opinion, he would be a better man on deck. He wanted a chance to do lookout. I agreed. He has very good eyes for lookout."

We were on our way northeastward, hunting a U-boat that a blimp thought she had crippled.

It was Sunday morning when we came up to the latitude and longitude where the crippled U-boat was supposed to be. The blimp had dropped some sort of buoy, and all hands were ordered to keep eyes peeled for it.

We could find no buoy. Our sound gear reported nothing all about but clean Atlantic Ocean.

A destroyer came out of the west and gave us "A! A!" on her signal searchlight, and then asked what we were doing. We said that we were hunting. "Hunt on," she said, and went slowly off. Then we saw a plane. Then a second plane. They were excited. An excited bomber can throw out emotion from every rivet. Larson, our Sparks, first class, came to the bridge with orders from the beach to open our radio direction finder and sail on the signal we would hear there. Somewhere ahead was a hovering bomber sending out radio signals. We tuned on the signals, altered course to the eastward, where they bore, and discovered that the destroyer was doing the same thing.

Over the destroyer the planes fluttered and wooed and pirouetted.

"Come on!" they seemed to say to her. "Hurry! Hurry, you waterbound, slow creature! Come on! Please come on!"

In the mid-afternoon the destroyer stopped. She was a small blue sliver standing still on the gray water ahead. The planes looked like gnats fluttering about her. We closed the miles, and then our sound gear found the submarine.

A plane dove swiftly and seemed to touch the sea. Then it soared up and away. She had stung the sea with something that spluttered and smoked. A smoke bomb. Plain as day, the gesture had said to the destroyer, "Here it is."

PORTRAIT OF A CHIUPA

By *Harrison Forman*. By wireless from Chungking[1]

The Chinese Army is made up of thousands of young men who in peacetime would be farmers or workers or students. The Chinese soldier today is fighting in his own country. He has seen the villages of his own people wiped out. He has seen the cruelty and ruthlessness of the enemy at firsthand. Time and again he has had to meet that enemy without adequate artillery or plane support. Yet because he knows that he is fighting for his freedom, he fights on with a courage and a will to win which deserve the highest admiration.

Li Pao-shan (pronounced Lee Bowshan) is a typical chiupa (pronounced jooba)—a Chinese doughboy or Tommy. He is a bright, eager farm lad; diligent, honest, possessed of amazing stamina and ability to undergo extreme hardships without complaining, with courage to challenge the hated Japanese in spite of their overwhelming arms, and beating them every time he has met them on anything like equal terms. Above all, Li Pao-shan has a sense of nationalism and appreciates what he is fighting for.

Li Pao-shan's three Yunnan friends, calling themselves, "three going to front youths," began a recruiting service with pleas through advertisements in the local newspaper: "We lose our homes, our work, our studies. We are driven

[1]From *The New York Times Magazine*, July 19, 1942. Copyright, 1942, The New York Times Company.

137

by thirst and hunger. Pain and distress afflict our daily lives. For all this none other than our race's enemy the Japanese are responsible. Unitedly should we marshal our resolute will to weather adversities, and we should with our brain and blood fight for final victory on the battlefield."

Coming of law-abiding peasantry, Li Pao-shan is sympathetically co-operative to native farmers in districts where he is stationed. The common bond contributes to closer relations wherein Li Pao-shan exchanges helpful farm hints, suggestions, and advice. Oftentimes he joins the farmer in putting these ideas to practical use, such as helping to install an improvement which results in betterment of the irrigation system or illustrating a different method of planting or of crop care. At harvest time Li Pao-shan and his comrades will frequently pitch in and help the farmers gather their crops, which service the grateful farmers repay with feasts and information of military value, all of which is knitting the country and its peoples closer together.

Li Pao-shan's camp life is simple. The camp itself is usually made of mat sheds wherein scores sleep together on one huge earthen platform called "the kang," which is heated from below through openings from the outside. His regular rations are two meals of rice or noodles daily, with two dishes of vegetables per meal to each table of eight. On garrison duty he supplements his fare by raising vegetables, pigs, chickens, rabbits, and goats. During hand-grenade practice, when grenades are hurled into a river or a lake, a squad is detailed to pick up the stunned or killed fish. His pay is only six Chinese dollars (the Chinese dollar is equal to about five cents in American money) monthly, but since he is not used to luxuries he does not require much more than the simple food and keep which the army supplies. He rises before dawn to the sound of bugles, then has an hour of exercise, which sometimes involves shadow boxing or, more often, merely trotting in a circle while shouting "Ee, er, san, shu" (One, two, three, four). After exercise, all assemble for the flag-raising ceremony, which is followed by the singing of the national anthem.

Reading and writing are taught, as well as elementary geography, history, and current events, which are interpreted and discussed.

Li Pao-shan has a fine sense of humor which is so lacking in his Japanese adversary. A favorite amusement on the Yellow River front is to taunt the enemy across the river with catcalls and insults until the exasperated Japanese open fire, whereupon Li Pao-shan and his comrades howl with glee from protected shelters at the display of temper, while at the same time appreciating in practical fashion that every shot expended by the enemy represents a contribution to the Chinese strategy of wearing the enemy down.

Another favorite stunt is the planting of partly camouflaged dummy airplanes, tanks, and artillery made of bamboo and paper, which the Japanese planes spot and bomb heavily. Jubilantly Li Pao-shan and his comrades rush from their shelters after the raid to gather up shrapnel, which they sell as junk to arsenals, thus having fun while earning pin money, furthering Japanese attrition, and contributing valuable metal for the manufacture of their own arms and ammunition. The young soldier also loves to annoy the Japanese with purposeful tricks such as flying kites over the Japanese lines, which, when released, scatter propaganda leaflets over the countryside.

Chiang Kai-shek has said, "Training is more important than fighting," wherefore considerable emphasis is placed not only on military but also on spiritual and political training. Li Pao-shan is drilled in the thought, "You are now soldiers of China, so think no more of your home or family, for we soldiers, at this critical juncture of our country's resistance against the aggressor, have no other home but battlefields."

Besides two lectures, he is daily given three field drills with special emphasis on bayonet usage—which is one reason why Li Pao-shan and his comrades have proved time and time again that they are, man for man, better fighters than the Japanese when once they are able to penetrate the Japanese protective screen of heavier arms and reduce fighting to hand-to-hand combat. Special training is given in the use of potato-masher hand grenades for anti-tank work, which, when tossed into a tank's caterpillar treads, will disable the whole vehicle.

Instruction is given as to which are the most vulnerable parts of Japanese supply trucks, such as gas tanks, the engine, tires, the driver. Since China must match the Japanese arms superiority with rapid changes of position, Li Pao-shan is trained in forced marching. He is an amazingly good walker. During the famous battle of Taierhchwang one Chinese column marched from four o'clock in the afternoon until eight o'clock in the morning, covering sixty miles, and immediately engaged and routed a surprised Japanese column.

Li Pao-shan's battle experience began almost from the first day he arrived at the front. There is an old Chinese saying that "Newborn calves do not fear tigers," hence eager fresh recruits are found most useful in attacks, though through recklessness they usually have proved easier targets than veterans, whose experience has taught them better use of cover from the enemy's fire.

Soon, indeed, Li Pao-shan saw Japanese at their very worst. He saw towns and villages ruthlessly destroyed, saw the tortured and mutilated bodies of luckless captives, the haggard, terrified faces of survivors, clearly bespeaking the awful ordeals to which they had been witness, while the blackened ruins of peasant homes where lay charred bodies offered the lie to a Japanese poster on the tottering wall near by which read, "The Japanese Imperial Army will not disturb the Chinese peasantry."

Once, Li Pao-shan's unit found itself cut off during an engagement. Calmly, his commander ordered the unit "to retreat" by advancing, for he knew the Japanese rear was always empty. Whereupon Li Pao-shan and his chiupa comrades became members of a ghost army of guerrillas, hundreds of whom are operating freely behind the Japanese lines, which actually run only along railways and highways with garrisons at strategic towns and bridges.

Li Pao-shan quickly learned that guerrillas try to oust Japanese from railways or highways, for they look upon these lines of communications as their principal sources of food supply, clothing, money, and, even more important, of arms. Example, a Japanese detachment of three or four thousand has upward of a hundred trucks shuttling between its base and its garrison outposts carrying ammunition, food, and gasoline. Glass spikes scattered along the road will halt a transport convoy and while the tires are being changed, guerrillas waiting in ambush pour withering machine-gun fire into the bewildered Japanese guards, finishing them off with grenades.

At other times Li Pao-shan and his band of fellow-guerrillas planted mines under the rail bed, then patiently sat down and waited until a Japanese supply train came along. When the train had been derailed, they swooped down and looted the twisted cars.

A favorite sport of Li Pao-shan and his buddies was to bait garrisons of Japanese who did not dare to leave their fortified shelters after dark. Night after night sham attacks were made, to which the frightened Japanese replied with furious fusillades until they were near collapse from tension and sleepless nights. They learned the guerrilla ghost army creed, which may be summarized as, "Withdraw when the enemy advances; harass him when he settles down; attack him when he is exhausted; give chase when he flees."

Li Pao-shan and his guerrilla companions enjoyed the complete confidence of the people. They traveled light and were fed, clothed, and protected by the lao pai shing (peasant masses). When the Japanese took the town of Shichiachwang, on the Peiping-Hankow railway where a narrow gauge branches off to Taiyuan, the farmers were angered at the conduct of the Japanese. They made contact with the guerrillas and formed a plan. Slim farmers dressed as attractive girls lured the Japanese to pursue them into an ambush, where Li Pao-shan and his buddies quietly did away with them.

Chinese army snipers, camouflaged with leaves, lie in wait for the Japanese enemy

Generalissimo and Madame Chiang Kai-shek with Lieutenant General Joseph W. Stilwell, commander of United States forces in China

Shipyards and factories in the "arsenal of democracy," working at new high speed, help to spell defeat for the Axis. Here a woman worker drills holes in a Hudson bomber belly gun door

Two United States Marines displaying a Japanese flag captured on Guadalcanal

The time Li Pao-shan spent with the ghost army until his unit once again was able to rejoin the ranks of the regulars gave him increased confidence in himself and in the ultimate victory of his country. Serving with the ghost army he saw the hated enemy when he was without his armor of tanks, planes, and artillery, and found him then far from invincible.

WINGING OVER THE WORLD

By *William L. White*[1]

The hum of the planes of the Ferry Command can be heard all over the world, for its job is to deliver anything that is badly needed anywhere. It sees that the planes pouring from factories in the United States and Canada get to the battle fronts. It brings back pilots to pick more planes off the assembly lines. It runs a passenger and a freight service. Sometimes you may find a woman in the pilot's seat of a ferry plane, for the Women's Auxiliary Ferry Squadron (WAFS) has been organized to ferry aircraft from factory to airdrome and release airmen for combat service. Mr. White introduces us to some of these ferry pilots who have been to the four far corners of the world and have had some exciting experiences.

A lean-faced major with quick black eyes leaned forward, elbows on table. "Tell you about one trip. I didn't know what I was getting into when the general said, 'You're leaving at seven tomorrow for Moscow via London.' Oumansky, the Russian Ambassador here, was going along, and in London we'd pick up Harry Hopkins and Lord Beaverbrook and Averell Harriman. About a hundred miles out I came down out of the soup—there was a 500-foot ceiling—and found I was right smack over a convoy. I don't know who was the most scared. They

[1] From *The Atlantic Monthly*, July, 1942, "To the Four Far Corners," by W. L. White. Copyright, 1942, The Atlantic Monthly Company.

scattered in every direction, afraid I was a dive bomber, and I scrambled back into the soup to avoid their fire.

"We didn't stay long in London—just long enough for my radio man to pick up the Russian signals; their alphabet has a few extra letters. Then we were off. But we ran into a whopping big cold front. I went high to avoid it and the temperature dropped to 25° below zero. Then something went wacky with the heater. They had rigged benches in the bomb bay for the passengers. I guess it was pretty dismal, huddled down in there, with no windows, and so cold they were miserable. That was one trip when nobody came up front to lean over the pilot's shoulder or maybe ask to sit in the co-pilot's seat for a while.

"Russian planes were to meet us six hundred miles out and escort us, and so far as we knew, we were right on schedule. But there was some mix-up, because at every airdrome Russian fighters came swarming up, and they meant business too. I was good and scared, so I just opened her wide and got out of there. We finally got her down on a Russian field."

"Say, George," said a blond pilot with very blue eyes. "That cold front over the sea—did you report it?"

"Sure. Why?"

"They ought to have a record of it. Weather's a kind of specialty of mine. When all this was first getting started they had me picking northern routes. We found icing conditions no one had ever heard of. In those days no two flights were alike.

"Never forget the first time I saw the Northern Lights. From a plane it's pretty gorgeous. But the spookiest thing is St. Elmo's fire. Sure, I know the professors tell you it's harmless. But they can have all of it. First a couple of purple sparks begin wiggling across your windshield like the ghosts of crazy angleworms not six inches from your nose. Then the stuff begins to gather into fiery doughnuts a foot thick at the tips of your propeller blades. Finally the nose of your plane is pushing along the purple and orange ghost of a medicine ball, and then you want to know who's saying it isn't dangerous—you up there alone, or some fellow in a swivel chair.

"But ice is the big hazard. You can pick up two or three tons before you know it. Also it can choke up your carburetor intake, and you feel your engines strangling for air. You've got to fly for your life, saying to yourself 'Why did I ever leave Texas?' Then pretty soon you find warm rain at low level and hear that nice sound the ice makes smacking back against your fuselage as it peels off the nose and wings, and you're glad you're a pilot again.

"It's all routine now. In the last year it's all been charted. We know what to expect anywhere any time of year. We've got the smartest weathermen on the job, and they're uncanny. If the weather man predicts high cirrus clouds two thousand miles out they'll be just where he says."

"There are very few weather problems in the tropics. What ice you ever find is so high you can always come down and wash it off. But watch out for tornadoes. I remember my first. All of a sudden—crackety-*bam*! A terrific burst of lightning, and the ship began to surge and fall in long billows of rough air. I didn't know what was up, but I got her off automatic pilot quick. It got rougher and rougher. Suddenly she zoomed from eight thousand feet to more than twelve thousand in less than a minute—a mile a minute elevator ride straight up— and immediately fell like a rock down to five thousand.

"I had a load of home-coming pilots. They should have been praying. Matter of fact they were all in a squirming pile, each one trying to get his parachute on. I don't know whether we were upside down or not—I was too busy trying to snatch at the controls. When we landed we found it had been a tornado with a ninety miles an hour ground wind. I figured that if that couldn't blow a B-24 to pieces nothing could."

"Tornadoes can be nasty," said the third pilot. "I tangled with one over the Java Sea. Started out to take Bill Bullitt to Cairo when Pearl Harbor changed everything—got orders to leave him in the Middle East and get on out to the Far East with three thousand pounds of machine-gun ammunition which they needed bad. And on the way I was to pick up an American general. At Rangoon I got my first look at the AVG crowd.

"The AVG's had been doing some tough fighting. The day the first Jap bomb smacked that field, every native servant vanished. You could see they didn't think it was their war. Both the British and AVG pilots were making their own beds, when they bothered to. Dinner consisted of knocking open a can of beans with a hand axe, and washing them down. Everything was piled high with dirty dishes.

"That afternoon the Japs came over, and the AVG's went up and showed me how. It was ten Jap bombers,

147

and it was as sweet and gentle as picking daisies. They'd got nine and just couldn't see how they'd been so careless as to let the tenth get away—they weren't kidding either.

"They told us to take the plane on down the Australian coast along with a lot of other American stuff they were assembling there. So I did, and next day the Japs came over and bagged the whole pile.

"When I had to tell the general they'd got his plane. . . . But all he said after a minute was, 'Well, the old girl had done her job.' I guess she had, too. Everywhere from the Arctic Circle to the Equator."

"Speaking of the Equator," said the first pilot, "you know that little weather post at that new airfield that's down under the Sahara? It's a good gang there, a couple of dozen, maybe, almost nuts for something to do. I promised 'em I'd see the next plane would bring 'em some baseball equipment."

"If you want to make a hit with a post in India," said the second pilot, "hide a few gallons of coca-cola syrup in your bomb bays. I took them five gallons but it was hardly a smell. They turned it over to the chaplain, and it was just enough to last the hospital a week. But they loved it."

"Reminds me of what happened in Egypt," said the third pilot. "They got a hankering for home-cooked food, so they taught a native to bake bread just the size of a hamburger roll. Then they bought an old water buffalo and ground it up, and they insist you couldn't tell them from hamburgers."

"I was in Iceland last week," said the fourth pilot, "and those guys sure bucked up. They'd just got their movie projector. Pretty soon they'll have one on every weather post all around the world, and we'll be rushing cans of film from field to field—but Iceland got going first. They were bragging that the world première of *Tarzan in New York* was held, not on Broadway or in Hollywood, but in Reykjavik. It's little things like that keeps their dobbers up."

"This whole ferry comand is just like a movie," said the first pilot. "We get a peek at all the wars, but then we're sent back home for another load. It's like watching a program of preview trailers and never getting to sit through the picture. That's the whole trouble with this job; none of us ever gets to see anything!"

He said it almost bitterly.

IF HITLER COULD SEE THESE

By *Sidney M. Shalett*[1]

At the Portland, Oregon, shipyards of Henry Kaiser the *Joseph N. Teal* was launched in September, 1942—the first ship in the world to hit the water ten days after keel-laying. At a big steel-and-wire company 408 new production records were made in the first six months of 1942. In Canada a power plant, larger even than the one at Boulder Dam, is well-nigh completed. And even as you read, these records may be broken. Day and night the "arsenal of democracy" is at work. To speed production and release men for the fighting fronts, thousands of girls and women have taken their places beside men on the production lines, in many cases doing work that women have never done before. They are riveting, making small parts of machines, putting fabric on non-stress areas of bomber wings, inspecting, filling shells, and assembling machine guns. Hundreds of workers have won recognition for new ideas for speeding up output. Mr. Shalett records the impressions of a trip made to more than sixty war plants in twenty-one cities six months after the United States entered the war.

Throughout the land a mighty revolution is in progress. American industry is beating the plowshares of peacetime—the autos, the electric refrigerators, the toasters, and the washing machines—into the swords of total war: planes, tanks, and high explosive bombs. It is a revolu-

[1]From *The New York Times Magazine*, July 12, 1942. Used with the permission of the author and *The New York Times*. Copyright, 1942, The New York Times Company.

tion to which there can be but one end: the doom of Nazidom.

American industry did not ask for this job of total conversion to production of the tools of war. It did not want it, any more than America wanted the war—any more than Americans wanted to exchange their cars for tanks. In many instances it was even slow to take up the task.

But now the colossus is at work, and the results of the gigantic effort are discernible in every manufacturing city in the land. You can see the planes and tanks and deadly bombs and you can grasp the inexorable promise of hundreds upon hundreds of thousands more ready to pour from the production lines. The Nazi propagandists may laugh and jeer and whistle in the wind, snorting "Fantastic!" and "Democratic lies!" just as long as it suits their fancy to do so. But the wave of American industrial might, built up by the free effort of a free and angry people, is going to mount up into a terrible deluge that will pour forth and wash out the ugly stains of brutality and oppression now upon the earth.

It is a thrilling thing to see American industry in action. In a way, it's a shame that military reasons make it impossible for every one in the land to have a look inside a few factories, for all the words and pictures and movies in the world can't quite capture and convey the feeling that a huge war plant in action can give you.

The clackety-clack of acres of machines, the rat-a-tat-tat of endless rivets being driven home, the fearsomeness of giant cranes swooping overhead, carrying planes, tanks, and mammoth caldrons of molten steel as if they were so many carpet tacks under a magnet; then the sight of the sleek, strong planes, the elephantine tanks with their deadly cannon-trunks, the millions of machine-gun bullets jumping from the machines like a plague of locusts—well, they make you feel better! They make you feel that you can stand up and cheer for your country, the country that is producing all this, and that you can wave the American flag, just as hard and as high as you please, without feeling in the least apologetic about it.

Did you ever see a million bullets under one section of one roof? Bullets are not especially pretty things, and, if you're an American, you'll probably prefer razor blades and lipsticks to cartridges any day. But, when you're in a war, and you see these million bullets and realize they're going to be used on your side, they're a mighty handsome sight!

When you stand in a Willow Run or a Chrysler tank arsenal, belief in your country's power becomes something more than wishful thinking. There is even a great deal to be said for the crack that hard-boiled "Charlie" Sorensen, production boss of Henry Ford's industrial empire, made when he became irritated at the restrictions the censors were trying to put on him in telling the story of Willow Run. Sweeping his fist to take in the incredible confines of the plant where the monster bombers are to be stamped out like Model T's, Sorensen exclaimed, "Bring the Germans and Japs in to see it. They'd blow their brains out!"

Everywhere along the tour of war plants, from Connecticut to Kansas (and, of course, in the many other States of the broad land that were not included in the

152

tour), factories exist that only a year ago still were occupied with civilian production, or, at best, were just beginning to get into war production.

Then, too, there were the factories that did not even exist one year ago and have sprung up miraculously like warriors from dragons' teeth—they are a story in themselves.

A plane winged over the flat, buffalo grass plains "somewhere in Kansas." The pilot, an official of an aircraft company, banked his ship and pointed down to a large, hangarlike building.

"There she is!" he exclaimed, shouting over the motor's roar. "Five weeks ago that was a wheat field. One Sunday the boss flew back from Dayton with the contract to build gliders for the Army. On Monday he bought that land—closed the deal by long-distance telephone with the owner, who was in California. Tuesday we broke ground. Now we're ready to start producing."

The manufacturers themselves are extremely confident of their ability to turn out as much war material as Uncle Sam and the United Nations will need. In general, their attitude may be summed up in the expression of W. W. Finlay, production chief at the vast Wright plane engine factory in the Cincinnati area. "If the United States and the agencies will just give us the materials," Mr. Finlay said, "they can call their own numbers."

The broad picture of production throughout the land is one that does credit to American industry. It is a picture that speaks well for industry's ability, ingenuity, and spirit. In every factory visited on the tour, there were dozens of examples of how brains had been put to work

153

to speed up production. Everywhere there were machines that cut to a matter of minutes jobs that formerly took hours to do.

In the spick-and-span, light, airy Wright engine factory in the Cincinnati area, pert Virginia Ritenour, wearing a blue cap, red sweater, and bright blue skirt, stood at the head of a machine—a whopper of a machine, 154 feet long.

"What do you do?" Virginia was asked. She replied, "I push a button."

Virginia neglected to add that when she pushed that button, it started an airplane cylinder head moving along a line that performed seventy-one operations, eliminating the work of thirty-nine old-style machines and reducing the number of operators required from thirty-nine to ten!

Right at present, however, America does not need to worry about machines cutting men out of jobs. Regardless of how many labor-saving devices are invented the war effort is requiring the hands of virtually as many able-bodied and skillful men and women as can be found.

The old idea of "skilled" mechanics has been practically outmoded. Obviously, there are not enough all-around skilled craftsmen to man the factories, so industry has broken down its operations to the point where one person just handles one small piece in the jigsaw puzzle of mass production.

"It used to take us two to three years to train a skilled worker to build an airplane," a manufacturer explained. "Now we train a thousand women in six weeks, each to do one of a thousand different jobs, and we build planes faster."

Also on the credit side in the ingenuity ledger is the way old machines have been retooled and put to work. As most of the reading public must know by now, you just can't take a set of tools and jigs and dies that once made auto engines and bodies and set them to work making airplanes. A lot of this machinery had to be scrapped or stored. It's a heartbreaking thing to see this. As Edsel Ford remarked, "The saddest thing in the world to me is the sight of a good machine standing idle." However, an incredibly large percentage of peacetime machines have been retooled and now are turning out shells, cartridges, and plane parts.

How about morale? The broad answer is: "In general, it's good—in some places, genuinely inspirational."

In the locker rooms and cafeteria of the St. Louis ordnance plant—another breath-takingly huge and beautifully designed modern arsenal—men and women workers were gathered in clusters, one hour before the mid-afternoon shift change. They were lounging, laughing, gossiping. "How about that?" a company official was asked. "Why are all these men and women in here loafing?"

"Loafing!" he laughed. "Why, they're not even on the job yet. You see, they like it here so well that hundreds of them come to work early, just to visit with each other a bit. It helps us—gets them on the job right on the button."

True, there were some spotty places in the picture. In a few of the factories and plants visited workers seemed indifferent and inclined to dawdle. In one Mid-western city a manufacturer said there were still some workers to whom the war meant merely an increased pay check. In another town there was an apparently well-substantiated report of a union that only recently had recognized the need for working overtime, even with extra pay.

However, in most places the workers really were bearing down, and it didn't look one bit as if they were just putting on an act. They paid no attention to visitors trooping through the plant. They have devoted large percentages of their incomes to the purchase of war bonds. They work days, nights, and Sundays, and some of them have gone for several months without taking a single day off from work.

When you stop and ask them what they think about the war, they look up from their machines and give you moving little answers—some emotional, some bloodthirsty, but all straight from the heart.

When Johnny Yukas in Pittsburgh tells you how he lost his brother Stevie on a destroyer and how he works at his machine now, praying with each turn of the wheel, "Let this gun get another German sub," the sudden stinging in your eyes tells you that Johnny Yukas means what he says. And when a blonde in slacks, working at a cartridge machine in the awesomely big St. Louis ordnance plant, demurely tells you that, as she turns out the bullets, she sings to herself in time with the clocking of the machine, "Kill-a-Jap, kill-a-Jap, kill-a-Jap," you're a little startled, but you know she means it too!

Another vastly inspiriting thing is the attitude of the industrialists themselves. For a long time in America it seemed fashionable to belittle industry and industrialists. As with labor, there were the exceptions among those encountered on the tour, but the majority of them were men who made it evident that they were doing jobs at which they were masters and that they were getting a tremendous lot of enjoyment out of doing them well. It was a joy to talk with some of the old-time shipbuilders and with some of the younger production men who now are making tanks and planes. It was a pleasure to hear rough-talking, tough-acting K. T. Keller of Chrysler growl, "Gimme a contract for a million of anything, and I can make it!" They left you with the distinct feeling that they are men who can and will do their jobs.

Another thing that made you feel pretty good was the way an Army ordnance major, on duty at a Pennsylvania tank plant, stopped and shook hands with a couple of dozen workmen on his tour of the plant, and the way Fred Geier, president of the Cincinnati Milling Machine Company—a model plant—knew the first name of practically every man in the vast shop. Somehow you couldn't imagine one of Hitler's monocled majors or one of his Rhineland "producers for the State" going through German factories under similar circumstances.

So it went, from the giant, whirling propellers at Hartford to the trainer planes of Wichita; from the aircraft carriers of Newport News to the "upsidedown" submarines at Manitowoc; from Ford's Willow Run to Pittsburgh's scorching steel mills. Production's booming, and the boom is just about ready to explode into a super-bang that is going to shatter the eardrums of Hitler, Hirohito, & Co. The days when American soldiers had to manoeuvre with kitchen wagons marked "This is a Tank" and gas pipes labeled "This is a Gun" are at an end. The

Arsenal of Democracy is now more than a phrase on paper.

The going still may be hard and bloody, and the end may not be yet at hand, but the picture of the Arsenal of Democracy at work is one from which every lover of freedom may draw courage and strength.

MARINES IN ACTION

By *Second Lieutenant H. L. Merillat*, United States
Marine Corps

For months the Japanese had been busily occupied in building bases on the Solomon Islands in the south Pacific from which they might go forth to new conquests or conveniently cut Allied communication lines to Australia. Then one day in August, 1942, they suffered a rude surprise. United States Marines went into action. This story, made public by the Navy Department of the United States, is from the report of what happened during the first days. It was written by a public-relations officer at the battle scene, where combined land, air, and sea forces were engaged. The hour designations used in the story conform to the 24-hour clock system which is used in the Navy. The 24-hour cycle runs from midnight to midnight.

Long before dawn on the 7th things were humming aboard the ships of the armada slipping silently into the passage between Guadalcanal and Florida Islands. Between 0200 and 0300 all hands turned out and wolfed a sumptuous breakfast. Who knew how long it would be before any of us had another real meal? Field rations would soon take the place of steaks and fried potatoes and scrambled eggs. Then we made our final preparations to go over the side and stood by, waiting for the eastern sky to brighten.

About dawn I went out on the deck of my transport. The weather had been on our side. Low clouds and mist had concealed our progress toward the Solomons all day the 6th. They had cleared during the night and the stars guided us on our way. At 0500 we could make out the dim outline of Guadalcanal to starboard. There was no sign of activity on the shore. At 0525 general quarters sounded, and the ship's crew took battle stations. At 0605 —"stand by to lower boats." Then came what all of us had been waiting tensely to see and hear; at 0607 a cruiser's gun boomed, and a salvo of shells landed in the laps of the Japs on Guadalcanal.

To the Japs on Guadalcanal and Tulagi it must have seemed that hell had broken loose. One laborer later taken as a prisoner said he thought he was dead. Salvo after salvo ripped into their midst. Navy planes unloaded high explosive and strafed the ground. The red trails of tracer bullets and shells cut the black coast of Guadalcanal. Fifteen miles to the north of us naval ships and aircraft were dealing out the same punishment to Tulagi.

At 0700 came the order to lower boats. Methodically they were swung out on their davits and lowered into the water. The ships bearing Marines who were to land in the first wave had already lowered away and soon the water about the transports was swarming with hundreds of speedy landing boats. New ramp landing and tank lighters were getting their first test in combat. Amphibious tractors, carrying engineering supplies, began their churning progress toward the beach, to be on hand when the speedier landing boats first hit the shore line.

0800 was "H-Hour" (attack hour) when the first wave of Marines landed on Tulagi. We could hear destroyers pumping high explosives into the beach. Then the barrage lifted and the Marines landed.

Meanwhile the landing boats were gathering for the assault on Guadalcanal. Proudly flying the Stars and Stripes the boats took on their loads of Marines and equipment and circled in the rendezvous area between the transports and the line of departure marked by two destroyers. I went in early, so I was on the water when the first wave hit the beach.

As our boat sped across the line of departure an amber flare from the shore announced that Combat Group A under Colonel L. P. Hunt had landed. We hit the beach about 1000 and learned that CG-A had landed without resistance. The beach presented a busy scene; already tank lighters were pulling up with their iron monsters. Amphibian tractors, which the Marines call "alligators," chugged ashore, equally at home on land or water. A steady stream of Marines was pouring out of boats. By 1045 Combat Group B, under Colonel C. B. Cates, was landing and lining up for its advance to the southwest. Scattered rifle shots marked the advance of the Marines as they fanned out through the tall grass and cocoanut groves.

We counted on the Japs arriving to bomb us about noon, figuring it would take that long for them to organize a flight of bombers in Rabaul and fly them down to Guadalcanal. Our guess was only a few hours off; in midafternoon bursting bombs and a sky full of Flak announced their arrival. Rising Sun bombers attacked our ships in the roads, without hitting any. Several were shot down. An hour and a half later the Japs attacked again with dive bombers this time. They hit one of our destroyers. Two more Japs were shot down.

That first day our advance was slow. There were no contacts with the enemy, for their whereabouts was unknown (we later learned they had scurried to the hills), and the thick tall grass and deep feeders of the Ilu River made a cautious advance imperative. At 1600 headquarters arrived on the shore and set up a command post in a palm grove south of the east branch of the Ilu. There we bivouacked for the night.

On the second day, August 8, the Marines on Guadalcanal pushed westward to take possession of the big new airfield which the Japs had obligingly built for us and to occupy and defend the area around Lunga Point. Combat Groups A and B completed the operation during the day, meeting no resistance until one group reached Kukum. There, south of the area occupied by the Marines, they ran into snipers and machine-guns in dugouts manned by the Japanese. The area was quickly mopped up, but nightly Jap patrols slip into our lines.

It became apparent after the first day that the Jap forces in the Lunga area had run to the hills when the American onslaught began on August 7. As we moved into their camps we found evidence that they had left in a hurry. Meals were still on the table, personal gear was tossed in all directions, valuable equipment was left intact. Ammunition dumps, pompoms, artillery, fuel, radio equipment, trucks, cars, refrigerating equipment, road-rollers, electric power plant—all were found just as the Japs had set them up and used them, except for the damage done by naval gunfire and bombing. A fine airport, with a runway 1400 yards long already completed, was almost ready to receive planes.

At noon on the 8th our visitors in the sky returned, this time bent on a daring raid. As our transports dispersed out to the open sea the Jap bombers came in. Almost skimming the waves, they lunged in among the transports and cargo ships. I was watching from the beach of Guadalcanal, and saw the big bombers burst into flames as they ran into murderous anti-aircraft fire from the ships. One, two, three—then I lost count in the confusion of the battle. Some ran the gauntlet of ack-ack and headed for the open sea, only to fall prey to our Navy fighters darting at them from high above. We heard that forty bombers had started on their mission; we heard that few returned to their base. Certainly their losses were enormous. In their suicidal raid over the strait they hit one of our transports. The Japs' second attempt to disrupt our operation had failed miserably.

The night of August 8 was one of alarms and excitement. We learned later that fighting was still continuing across the straits in the Tulagi area. In Guadalcanal it was a sleepless night for other reasons. First, the rain came, in a drizzle, then in torrents. Everyone and his gear was thoroughly drenched. Trying to get a cat nap in our puddles of water, we were aroused by a thunderous bombardment. Out at sea to the west, the big guns spoke. Flashes of light told us that a naval battle was in progress. We do not yet know the full story of that battle but we do know that the Jap ships were turned back—ships which undoubtedly had slipped toward Guadalcanal and Tulagi to blast us by night, to sink our transports and supply ships and bombard our forces on land. The Japs' third determined attempt to knock us out had failed.

Our comrades in the Tulagi area have had a tough fight. The Japs there—cut off from escape, well dug in, and strongly armed—fought from their fortresses to the last man. Brigadier General William H. Rupertus, assistant commander of our forces who directed the operation in that area described the battle as "the most wonderful work we have had in history." Hundreds of Marines became heroes and veterans in the bitter fighting.

The first wave of the raider battalion, under the command of Colonel Merritt Edson, hit the beach in the northwest end of Tulagi. It is a hilly wooded area, and the Marines expected tough going. The Japs apparently expected no landing, however, and offered no opposition, on the beach. One man was lost by a sniper's bullet, the rest landed safely. Avoiding the trails along the shore which were commanded by steep cliffs, the raiders made their way along both sides of the central ridge of the little island, pushing through dense brush and woods. In two hours and a half they covered a mile and a half, from the beach to the southeast. Then the shooting started.

The Marines came up against a strongly defended hill where a concentration of machine-gun nests held them up for an hour. The battle was joined at short range, with Marines sneaking up on nests of Japs concealed in caves and crawling down the steep cliffs to drop hand grenades into the cliff holes. A company on the north side of the island pushed through strong opposition and took the ridge above the playing ground. The Japs allowed them to pass through, then opened up from the rear. Snipers in trees, behind rocks, concealed in buildings, harassed the Marines.

In the morning the Marines resumed the offensive. Two companies which had mopped up the northwest end of the island upon landing the first day, advanced southward. On the second day they pushed through from the beach west of the playing ground. That gave the Marines positions for mortars and machine guns on three sides of the main Jap position. By 1500 they had blasted the Japs out of their strongholds and completed physical possession of the island. That was not the end of the story, however, for snipers were still concealed in trees, tall grass, and caves. Twice the next day Marines combed the area, finding snipers each time.

Not one of the hundreds of Japanese on the island surrendered. They had to be blasted out of each position. Their defense was built around small groups in dugouts and caves, communicating with each other by radio. In many of the cliffside strongholds radios were found. In one case, on the third day, a Jap was still firing from his deep cavern after all his comrades had been shot. For two days he had lived without food or water. Three Japs cornered fired until they had only three rounds for one pistol. Then one of them killed his two companions and turned the gun on himself. Some caves were manned by thirty or forty Japs. When the one manning the machine gun was picked off, another would take his place, and so on till the last man was dead.

The assault on Gavutu, mile-long island which was the site of the principal Japanese seaplane base in the Solomons began at 1200 on the 7th. In the dawn bombing raid all the planes based there had been blasted.

As noon drew near, the landing boats approached Gavutu from the shore of Florida island. Even before the assault wave had formed, the Japs opened up with a rain of fire from their hill fortress. The Marines came in under this fire. They had hoped to land on the concrete seaplane slips, but the naval gunfire and bombing had hurled huge blocks of concrete into the water, blocking the approach.

The attacking Marines had to clamber on to a wharf higher than their boats, swept by machine gun fire. Major Robert H. Williams, their commanding officer, was badly wounded leading his men in the first wave and had to be evacuated.

Captain George Stallings took command and led the attack which wiped the Japanese from Gavutu.

On Gavutu is a hill 148 feet high which the Japanese had converted into a honeycomb of cavern emplácements; tunnels connected many and some rock-hewn chambers were 20 by 20 feet. The hill rises steeply from the flat strip near the beach and from the mouths of scores of caves the Japs poured down a withering fire. Many Marines showed great courage that day in assaulting the formidable stronghold. Captain Harry L. Torgersen, for example, covered only by the fire of four of his men, rushed from cave to cave, hurling into them charges of TNT tied to boards with short fuses. By himself he closed up more than fifty of the pest holes and came out of his daring day's work with only a wrist watch broken and his pants blasted off.

Platoon Sergeant Harry M. Tully, who had seen many of his best friends shot down in the first blast of machine-gun fire from the cliff, for two days and nights operated as a lone wolf, surpassing the Japs in cunning and patience, picking them off one by one after lying in wait for long periods. From Gavutu he picked out machine gunners on Tanambogo, 500 yards away, and shot them down. By night he sat on the beach, watching the water for tell-tale traces of Japs as they swam into the beach behind logs. Once he watched a log float to the beach only six feet from where he lay in wait. The Jap did not stir for eighteen minutes, nor did Sergeant Tully. Then the Jap lifted his head and Tully shot him.

In a sense it is wrong to mention heroes by name for not all heroes can be named and to omit them seems to derogate from their courage and brave deeds. There were so many heroes in the assaults on Tulagi, Gavutu, and Guadalcanal that not all can be named, and not all will ever be known.

In two days of bitter fighting the Marines cleaned out the Japs on Gavutu. In the afternoon of August 7, even before their conquest was complete, the Marines ran up the Stars and Stripes from the hilltop on Gavutu. The bugle blew colors, and the Marines paused long enough to cheer the raising of our flag on Jap-held territory. The Rising Sun still floated over Tanambogo, half a mile away, but the Marines shot it down, leaving Old Glory as the sole flag waving at dusk over that once strong Japanese base.

LIFE IN A LIFEBOAT

By *Chanler A. Chapman*[1]

There have been many harrowing stories by those who have
been on torpedoed ships. This is not such a one. Its author, a
son of the late scholar-poet John Jay Chapman, was on his way
to North Africa to drive an American Field Service ambulance
when the enemy struck. A lover of boats and the sea, he found
his eight days on a lifeboat a new and thrilling adventure. His
story, which begins immediately after the U-boat attack, is a
fine sample of the invincible spirit which is part of the heritage
of free men.

I went forward along the starboard side and noticed a
launched lifeboat in the water in charge of Mr. Barton,
second officer, twenty-three years old, nine years at sea
and never torpedoed before. Then I did a fairly selfish
thing. I went back to my cabin, picked up a fisherman's
hat and my pair of sneakers. I thought the sneakers and
hat would be obligatory if we were going to bat about
within nine degrees of the Equator in an open boat. I
tossed the shoes and hat into the lifeboat and started to
obey Mr. Barton's command to jump. Though I did not
have far to jump, I hesitated. Mr. Barton roared, "Jump."
I finally relaxed and just sort of squatted down and pitched
forward and precipitated myself onto the arms, heads and
laps of people in the stern of an already crowded lifeboat.
We shoved off to get clear of the ship before she finally
went under.

[1]From *Life*, September 28, 1942. Copyright, 1942, Time, Inc.

Within no time at all the sub herself appeared, quite a long way off, and we ignored her. It was more vital to us to watch our own vessel going down. On the wreckage and packing cases were two or three men balancing themselves. One man kept blowing on a whistle attached to his life jacket. He was as persistent as a tree toad in spring.

We headed in among the wreckage, taking pains not to be swamped by various heavy cases which were barging about in the swell. We picked up two of our mates and then noticed the sub was in our midst, no longer just a conning tower, but fully surfaced. When we first saw the conning tower we thought they might possibly machine-gun us. Now we saw her pick up two members of our crew. One of these was burned by steam and had scalds and one eye was closed. Give the devil his due, they dressed this man's wounds and put a patch over his eye and returned him and a deckhand to us. They were as arrogant as a fish hawk among new-hatched chicks—polite, sure, young and merciless, but they gave us our course and we were glad to be rid of them. Then started the long week and a day to shore, in a lifeboat.

It took our ship about seven minutes to go down. I immediately transferred my sandals and bathing shorts to a fireman who was clothed only in a life preserver. He was the whistler from among the packing cases. I also gave him one of my two safety pins which attached my long woolens to my life preserver. He needed this to keep his new pants up. The other pin I kept and used for many purposes during the rest of the trip.

Mr. Barton had us row to a life raft which had come adrift from the wreckage. As it was very crowded in the boat, some of us, including myself, volunteered to sit on the raft and be towed. It was agreed not to cast us adrift and to give us a chance to come back to the lifeboat if that seemed the best plan. The raft was a heavenly place because there were only six or seven of us on it and the thing was made to hold fourteen. By contrast it was like a comfortable club. We began getting out our stanchions and stretching canvas about the sides and an awning overhead. In the meantime, the lifeboat had hoisted its cherry-red Latine mainsail and jib and was attempting to tow us. This was not successful. We made next to no progress.

In a couple of hours Mr. Barton issued two small pieces of chocolate to each of us and a small tot of water, probably only one ounce, just a drop. This surprised and delighted me, because the boatswain, who was not in our boat, told me a couple of weeks before that if we took to the lifeboats we would not get anything to eat or drink for twenty-four hours. It was not that way in our boat.

Late that afternoon Mr. Barton made us come aboard the lifeboat, to which we transferred the raft rations and water, paddles and bright yellow awning. We hated to give up our comfortable, luxurious raft, but we did what Barton said without grumbling and joined the overcrowded, jabbering *hoi polloi* on the lifeboat.

As darkness descended, Barton asked who could help him steer and sail the boat. This was my chance. I had told him about crossing the North Atlantic on the 47-ft. ketch *Shanghai* and getting wrecked off Nova Scotia eighteen years ago. He thought it a little insane that five men should want to sail across the North Atlantic in a small boat just for fun. But now it was the best kind of medicine both for him and me.

I asked to be allowed to take the 4-to-8 watch on a four hours on, eight hours off basis, and he accepted the offer. This was a godsend. It meant eight hours' work every day, the kind of work I love best of all because you have next to no intellectual strain. You sit in the stern sheets of a double-ended lifeboat, before dawn and before sunset, every day, with the tiller under the right or left arm, according to which tack you are on. The northeast trades are behind you. From time to time you are becalmed. That is the worst. The rest of the time you go slithering down endless hills and valleys of hard, salt water, black at night but by day a brilliant cruel blue. The boat is low in the water. I don't think she had over twenty inches of freeboard. When the weather is a little rough or squally or the boat gets a little crossed up against a whitecap, one side or the other will ship a little water. This produces protests from the sitting, squatting, hunched-up humans on that particular side. When the wind or the course is shifted so that there is a risk of jibbing, the annoyance is even greater. One has to wake up the mass of sleepers on the bottom, sides, and thwarts of the boat and get them to row a few strokes on the starboard or port side. This they do slowly. There is not much danger either from swamping or from snapping the little mast out of her in a sudden squall. This latter would be really bad, yet one hates to shorten sail when the going is strong and favorable. We only did it once, and we were sorry we did it that time.

It is like endlessly coasting on and on over endless hills

171

with full control in the tiller and the mainsheet which is worked without benefit of blocks or pulleys. The 4-to-8 watch is the best in the world. It is always broken by the morning and evening meal at 6 A.M. and 6 P.M. At our first morning meal we each got one ounce of water. Because of its greasy saltiness we ate very little pemmican and only moderate quantities of malted milk, chocolate or biscuit with it.

Barton explained why this short ration of water would be necessary. We might possibly be in that lifeboat from twenty to thirty days. We thought we were between 450 and 650 miles from land. There was neither sextant, chronometer nor log. There was a two-shilling Mercator's projection of the entire world without any names on it. We knew that the Brazil Current would join the Equatorial Current and carry us north and west along the coast of South America. Therefore we kept steadily to the southwest and southwest by south. Our greatest fear was that we should be carried past Trinidad and Tobago and the Windward Islands and somehow get into the Caribbean Sea and have to go clear across to Cuba or even to Yucatan before we got to land. That would have been bad. That is why we wanted to hit any part of South America, any old stretch of mud or mango swamp rather than be carried on indefinitely in our crowded, thirsty cockle.

At noon we had another meal with another ounce of water. Noon was usually bad because it was really hot. That is where the Abdol vitamin tablets came in strong. They were pliant and could be swallowed without using any saliva or moisture. When you put an ounce of water

172

on top of one, you could feel the old food values reaching out into your system and nourishing you.

By 8 or 9 o'clock in the morning various oars and stanchions and paddles were rigged to support the canvas awning. We had eight cotton blankets that sometimes were placed on top of the awning to produce a deeper shade. In any case there never was room for all parts of all the people to be under the awning at the same time. The people in the bow had a smaller awning of their own, but it also was insufficient. The smaller boys and men slept in the bilges, curled up under benches, sometimes with their legs higher than their heads. It lasted for days. It was not too bad. Nobody went bats.

One of the best things about being on the navigating staff was that better sleeping arrangements were afforded us. A man cannot watch a compass, the wind, sail and sea and, at night, perhaps a star for four hours if he is half asleep. So we of the staff were allowed to stretch out straight. I got so that I could bite off sleep like a man eating bananas. As a rule I can use a good deal of sleep. I got a good deal of it in the lifeboat.

The two things I liked best about the trip were learning to get along on very little water and sailing the lifeboat. I think Barton really thought me a little odd when after four or five days I still told him from time to time and in confidence that I liked nothing better in the world than sending that swell little cockle shooting down those endless waves with the twenty-four of us in her really going somewhere. That was the kind of race that counted.

A CANADIAN DESTROYER MEETS
THE WOLF PACK

By *Charles Rawlings*[1]

In 1939 *Skeena*, bright and shining, welcomed Their Majesties, the King and Queen, to Canada. Later she carried the Royal Party to Prince Edward Island, and the King lived on her bridge for hours at a time, his Royal Standard above him at her gaff. With the coming of war she put on the battle paint of the North Atlantic. She arrived in England the first day of Dunkirk and lived through action there for a year, later returning to Canada to help guard the western buttress of that great overseas bridge of ships known as the Western Ocean Convoy. Here is part of *Skeena's* story.

This is a Navy tale of convoy. The ensigns of a dozen nations fly and some of them go down in its action. Its setting is outside in the middle longitudes of the North Atlantic Ocean, and they belong to no land, but it is a Canadian story.

A thin screen of Canadian ships faced Hitler's undersea wolf pack attacking in great force out there and brought their convoy through; battered, decimated, bloody, but on the course, steaming home in line of convoy still. It is known, where such things can be known and talked, as *Skeena's* story—*Skeena* the destroyer. She was not alone. She had supporting corvettes, those plump,

[1]From *Maclean's Magazine*, March 15, 1942. Excerpts from "Fighting Ships." Used with permission of the Maclean Publishing Co., Limited, Toronto.

small, tumbling ship clowns in the Battle of the Atlantic's grim circus, and they fought like lions. She had S.C.X. under her lee, Slow Convoy X, and it was a brave convoy manned by brave men who kept their weary merchantmen plodding on through more than two days and two nights of sustained *Rudelsystem* attack, as the Germans call it. But it is *Skeena's* story as you will see.

The men on *Skeena* made rendezvous with S.C.X. and saw that it was a big convoy, sixty-odd bottoms. They studied it quietly, unemotionally, marvelling mildly, if at all, at its size in contrast with their own. It was like all the other convoys of the past war years—a trifle more weather-beaten, possibly, for each one as it came to them was a little older. It was stretched out as far as a hoisted signal could be seen, and there were flush deckers there and three island freighters, and tankers and squat-rigged modern hulls all gear and hatches, and tall rigged old coasters, and a snub-nosed laker with her funnel seeming to pop up out of her very transom like a shanty stovepipe. They wallowed slowly ahead rolling out their vulnerable thin-plated, heavy bellies.

Making those bellies heavy was a half million odd tons of precious stuff to nurture and strengthen Britain in her island fortress. In the cold, greasy forecastles, or manning their faithful engines and their decks, were men like themselves, men of the sea, enough of them to people a small village; 2,500 more or less, officers and men of the merchant navy.

The bunting signals went aloft on the commodore's flagship, just one of the merchantmen chosen as lay leader of the caravan. The western escort that had

175

brought the convoy out from Canada, answered and departed. *Skeena* motioned her corvettes, and they took station. She made a short run off the convoy's flank and looked ahead and to the south, taking a wary scent of sea and sky. What lurked out there? Nothing? Who knew? *Skeena* turned and slid back and took her lead station.

Where they were at this particular moment does not matter, for the whole North Atlantic Ocean was preparing right then to be exactly the same all over. A gale struck. In three hours it hove them to, escort and convoy alike. They lay, heads tucked under wing or heads tucked under stern whichever way their widely different hulls could best lay to. With engines just holding way they tussled with an old and honourable enemy. In thirty-six hours it decided they had had enough and could go on. All shipshape and on station, the great caravan set off on a course that carried them north and east until they sighted a bold headland of basalt mountain and glacier and stark shore cliffs. It was a bright day with a long dead following sea heaving them along, and all hands came up into the morning sunlight to stare at the strange cold cape.

"Torpedo! Starboard bow!"

It was the first shout of all the shouting that was to follow. The first warning cry. *Skeena*, far ahead at the front of the fleet, closed at twenty-four knots.

"That way!" the right wing ships cried to her. "Periscope! Torpedo! Something! It sank and is gone."

She followed their pointing arms and searched and listened with those long mysterious tentacle ears called

Asdic that can hear beneath the water farther than any shark can hear or eavesdropping cod down on the bottom mouthing his thick lips. Nothing! *Skeena* turned and surveyed the convoy drawn ahead. It had no vacant station, no limping ship.

"Break silence only if you see and are sure of what you see," she ordered. "That—why, that was nothing."

Nothing it remained for an hour. A short crisp message broke the air. It came from the Commander in Chief, Western Approaches.

"Enemy in your vicinity," it said.

The commodore heard it and could read its official code. *Skeena*, too. Together they decided to change course, and the great flotilla, still unaware, made its swing and settled down due north with the icy coast abeam, forty miles. The evening, late and lingering in those latitudes, came drifting down. Sunset tinted the white mountains rosy pink.

At 9.37, just good dark, a warhead blew the belly out of the fourth ship in the port wing, and she went down in the moonlight like a stone with all hands. The next ship in the line signalled the attack with white rockets. *Kenogami*, one of the corvettes who was nearest, carried out a sweep in the rear of the convoy, and at 9.42 she was heard to drop a single depth charge. At 9.48 she sighted a torpedo track that passed her starboard bow, and at 9.50 she sighted a U-boat at 1,000 yards steaming away at high speed. She opened fire with her four-inch guns but she needed more light on the target, and at ten o'clock she lost all contact. *Skeena*, near her now, illuminated the port side of the convoy by star shell, and realizing *Kenogami* had lost contact, ordered her to search for ten minutes and then come back. When returning herself, the commodore far in the front of the convoy reported to her that he had sighted a U-boat on his port bow very close to the time of the opening explosion. He thought there must be two Huns attacking. At 10.10 two merchantmen sighted what was considered to be a third submarine, and within a few more moments four ships were crying out by megaphone and firing machine-gun tracer at a U-boat that was inside the convoy running down between the seventh and eighth columns. *Skeena* thought of ramming, but when this proved impossible owing to the number of ships in the way, she again fired star shell and closed the position and dropped depth charges. After twenty minutes another sinking called her away, and one minute later a tanker exploded.

The moon was still aloft but hard and white now, coldly staring down. Overhead the aurora had flamed into wild pastel, orange and electric-blue and crimson. The moonlight was hard on the white mountains. All warmth had left the sky, had left the world. It was what it had been all the time, a battle place, and the enemy was not one, or two lurking submarines. It was the wolf pack. Naval headquarters estimates the attacking force at this time at twelve submarines.

Shortly after midnight a cloud bank mercifully moved in from the northeast and covered the mocking moon. The aurora flickered and went out. In the first of the darkness that seemed like the blackness of a pit, there were shouts and then suddenly the jangle of machine guns spitting white hot tracer.

178

"Here!"—"Here's the swine!"

Skeena was close enough to hear, and she swung into the convoy and raced down lane to ram. The submarine crossed her too far ahead, and, like a ki-yi-yi-ing dog in flight, it skidded around a corner and raced up the next lane over. They passed going in opposite directions and *Skeena* could see the wet conning tower of the Hun shining in the darkness and, as she watched, it slid under in a crash dive. At that moment the convoy, acting on orders from the commodore who had full charge of ordering such manœuvres, made an emergency turn to port, and *Skeena*, caught in the changing traffic, was suddenly surrounded with danger of collision. Her people say that it was the direst moment of all the night. In the absolute darkness, where to turn? She knew one thing sure—she of all of them must not be put out of action that night. A black hulk leaped out of the darkness— one of the merchantmen—and just in time the 32,000 horse-power in her engines reared her back and away in full reverse. Then she wheeled and drove on and on until at last she was free and the convoy was inside of her, and outside was nothing but darkness and sea and enemy. While she was still sweat-soaked and panting from the terror, the ship nearest her, a tanker carrying fuel oil, exploded. It shot an orange geyser of flame a hundred feet into the black sky.

At last ... morning and the sun.

Skeena's commander slouched down in his chart-room chair, boots stretched out, and stared far away into the coming night. It was time for plans. They would have to be his plans.

At noon he killed. The wolf pack teased a hard-luck ship, or made a bet, or in their humourless way, ordered a single U-boat to try a desperate sneak attack. It caught a ship named *Thistle Glen* and hit her amidships with one powerful warhead. And then, not satisfied at the mere sound of the well-aimed shot going home, it stuck its periscope out to have a gander.

"Periscope!" raised the cry.

Skeena closing fast was close enough to look. It was a light grey periscope, sneaking slowly under. There was no need for instruments to divine range and depth. Pounce attack! Ten depth charges, 5,000 pounds of TNT with shallow fuse settings, blasted the water into geysers which sloshed back to make a patterned doily of foam. *Skeena* drew off to 1,700 yards and those long mystic ears, the Asdic, groped and found him. He was on the bottom frozen with terror, wounded more or less. This time slowly, with check and counter-check of every move, with engines slowly turning and the detection routine going on as still and studied as in an examination drill, the exact spot where he lay on the seas floor was found.

"Object bearing red forty-five, sir," said Lieutenant Wilcox, binoculars fast to eyes. "Appears to be a destroyer. Yes! A destroyer! No! Two destroyers! Three destroyers! Three destroyers, sir! Four destroyers! Five destroyers!"

They were fanned out wide on the horizon, sweeping westward. As he watched, the outside specks closed in, for the flotilla had sighted him. They changed from black to grey. Their spars became distinct from their funnels. The white tulle at their bows ravelled steadily away. Their leader closed with *Skeena* and hailed through the loud hailer. It asked questions of technic. What screen had they been using? It asked that. What night technic? Quickly it asked and seemed to jerk the answers inboard as if they were something sprawling scandalously in mid-air. There was no compassion, no mercy in that bloodless, nettled voice.

"When did this begin?" it snapped.

Skeena told him.

There was a pause. The air, the strip of sea between the two ships seemed to hold still for a long eloquent moment. Then the voice, human now, gentle with understanding, said,

"I did not know that it had been as bad as that."